Simon Nelson Patten

Premises of Political Economy

Being a Re-Examination of Certain Fundamental Principles of...

Simon Nelson Patten

Premises of Political Economy
Being a Re-Examination of Certain Fundamental Principles of...

ISBN/EAN: 9783337073213

Printed in Europe, USA, Canada, Australia, Japan

Cover: Foto ©Suzi / pixelio.de

More available books at **www.hansebooks.com**

THE

PREMISES OF POLITICAL ECONOMY;

BEING A

RE-EXAMINATION OF CERTAIN FUNDAMENTAL PRINCIPLES

OF

ECONOMIC SCIENCE.

BY

SIMON N. PATTEN, Ph.D. (Halle).

PHILADELPHIA:

J. B. LIPPINCOTT COMPANY.

1885.

Dedication.

CONTENTS.

	PAGE
INTRODUCTION	7

CHAPTER

I.—RENT	19
II.—THE SOCIAL CAUSES PRODUCING A HIGH PRICE OF FOOD	46
III.—THE LAW OF POPULATION	72
IV.—THE RELATION OF RENT TO WAGES . . .	95
V.—FREE COMPETITION	121
VI.—THE LAW OF DIMINISHING RETURNS . .	152
VII.—FREE-TRADE	184
VIII.—THE MEANS OF MAINTAINING A HIGH STANDARD OF LIFE	211

5

CONTENTS

INTRODUCTION.

THE Science of Economics has had a historical development. At first some of its important truths were dimly perceived, then a theory was formulated, new doctrines from time to time were added, the old doctrines gradually became better known and understood, and errors have been gradually detected and discarded. As a result of this development the doctrines of the science have been formulated in a very objectionable manner, and economic truths have lacked symmetry, the newer doctrines not having been applied to all parts of the science, while old errors, though driven from their strongholds, still lurk in many unsuspected corners. These considerations make a return to the discussion of first principles. necessary, and this I take up the more readily because of a conviction that they are not correctly apprehended in the current economic literature.

Since the time of Ricardo the discussion of first principles has been very one-sided, the ultimate premises used by him having been accepted by most subsequent writers. It is true that many economists have rejected the premises of Ricardo, but having done this on other than purely economic grounds, they have had little or no effect on the development of the science. It is my purpose in the following discussion to contest from strictly economic grounds the validity of several fundamental propositions laid down by Ricardo and other writers of the same school.

A word of explanation is necessary to prevent an erroneous conception of my purpose. I do not call in question those ultimate facts concerning the physical conditions of external nature of which Ricardo makes so much use, and on which deductive Economics is at present based, but shall endeavor, by the use of other facts equally ultimate in their nature, to prove that many of the leading doctrines now accepted by most economists must be discarded, to give place to other doctrines more in harmony with the real phenomena.

An illustration from natural science will make clear what I have in view. The motion of the earth around the sun is the result of two separate forces, either of which operating alone would produce a far different result. If gravitation were the only operating force, the earth would fall into the sun, but if the first law of motion alone prevailed, the earth would fly away into empty space. If only one of these forces, as gravitation, were known, men would predict the destruction of the earth by fire as a fact of the near future, and those who denied this, as inconsistent with the kindly purposes of Providence or what not, would be regarded as unscientific, and derided for bringing in other than physical causes to account for the phenomena of nature.

The justice of these charges would entirely depend upon the method pursued by the objectors. If they denied the law of gravitation, the charge would be just; but if they sought to demonstrate the existence of natural laws that counteracted gravitation, and thus to prove false the conclusions based on the assumption that gravitation were the only operating force, then they would be pursuing a proper course of investigation, and could not justly be stigmatized as unscientific.

The present Science of Economics is as imperfect as Astronomy would be if one of the laws of motion were unknown. In each department of Economics all the deductions are based on some one ultimate fact, and the conclusions arrived at are true only on condition that no other ultimate facts exist which influence the phenomena under investigation. The law of rent is usually discussed as though differences of soil were the sole cause of rent, and the law of population only considers the difference between the possible rates of increase of population and food, while free trade and the effects of free competition are discussed from an equally narrow stand-point. It is plain that such discussions are of a very limited value, if many ultimate facts, or even any, are overlooked, and it is my purpose to point out these neglected facts, and to place them in proper relation to those facts at present so much used in deductive Economics.

The increase in the price of food accompanying the advance of civilization, is the main point which economic theories have to explain. Is the increased price the result of a single cause, or does it arise from a combination of various causes, and are these causes of a physical or of a social nature? The well-known answer of Ricardo is that there is a single physical cause,—the various degrees of fertility which different lands possess. The best lands are limited in quantity, and as the demand for food increases less fertile lands, having a higher cost of cultivation, must be brought into use, and hence the price of food must rise when more food is required for an increasing population. Ricardo gives this answer in his explanation of rent, and Malthus adopts the same view in discussing the law of population, by assuming that the means of subsistence are exhausted, or nearly so, because the price of food is high. It is no wonder that so simple and apparently self-evident an explanation has found ready acceptance, and one theory of rent having been presented, no one took the trouble to investigate whether some other theory could account for all the facts needing explanation.

In the following chapters I shall endeavor to present a consistent theory, showing that the main causes of rent, and of the increased price of agricultural produce, are not of a physical, but of a social nature. The prevalence of ignorance, and a lack of appreciation of inexclusive pleasures, cause a demand for commodities of which nature can supply but small quantities, waste a large part of what is produced, and at the same time prevent the distribution of population and the increase of capital. The ignorant and inefficient classes displace the skilled and intelligent, because their wants are so limited that they are able to give a greater surplus as rent than the higher classes can do, and whatever class can give the greater surplus gets possession of the field of employment, and thus the survival of other classes is prevented. By these social causes a high price of food can be brought about, but this high price affords no indication of the exhaustion of the food-supply, unless the field of employment is much larger to the ignorant than to the intelligent classes. From the nature of the field of employment, then, must it be determined whether rent has physical or social causes. If the field of employment enlarges as the people become skilled and accumulate wealth, then what may be called the social theory of rent is correct;

on the other hand, if the ignorant possess much the larger field of employment, then the physical theory of rent based on the natural obstacles to the increase of food must be accepted. The only condition on which it could be true that the field of employment would be larger to the ignorant than to the intelligent classes, is that the greater portion of the land of the earth has so low a degree of fertility that the higher classes cannot be employed on it. If the greater part of the land has, or can be made to have, a high degree of fertility, there can be no doubt that the intelligent classes, when not prevented by social causes, can obtain a much larger gross produce from the more fertile land, and, while supporting a much larger population, can also increase the average return for labor above what the inefficient classes could get from all the land. Whether the physical or social theory of rent is correct must be determined by the ratio of the superior to the inferior lands, and if I show that most of the land either has, or is capable of having a high degree of fertility, I shall disprove the physical theory of rent, which explains the increased price of agricultural produce from physical causes.

The difference between the view of nature which Ricardo tacitly adopts and that which I advocate may be well illustrated in the following manner. Suppose the bed of a lake, like that of Lake Michigan, to be gradually filled with water, how could its depth at any given point be determined? Ricardo, if he reasoned as he does in solving the problem of rent, would answer that the depth at any point could be discovered by determining how much the water had risen since the point in question was submerged.

Now this method of procedure overlooks the effect of the water on the lake's bed. The depth at various places has been changed by the currents in the water and by the action of the waves. The outline of the bed of Lake Michigan is very different from what it was when first filled with water, and no knowledge of its old outline will enable us to determine deductively the outline of the present bed.

Most of the conclusions drawn from the law of rent . are defective, because it is assumed, first, that land is thrown out of cultivation, when less land is needed, in an order exactly the reverse of that in which it is brought into cultivation,—the last land brought into that cultivation being the first to be thrown out; and, secondly, the rise of rent since land of a given quality has been brought into cultivation is a correct index of the rent that could be paid for the land. The extent and character of the field of employment sets a limit to the support of population, and fixes the average return for labor; and if this field of employment, besides being determined by external nature, is also influenced by

2

the skill and intelligence of the laborers, just as the bed of a lake is changed by the action of the water within it, then the influence of the different civilizations upon the field of employment must be determined before it can be known how an increase of population will affect the average return for labor. I shall especially strive to show that, as the law of rent has not been correctly apprehended, the field of employment enlarges when the intelligence and efficiency of labor is increased, and that the highest average return for labor is compatible with the greatest possible population; while, on the other hand, whatever diminishes the average return for labor also limits the field of employment so that only a smaller population than before can be supported.

The real cause of the present social distress is to be found in the prevailing sentiment regarding the consumption of wealth, and especially of food. Nature is not equally productive of all kinds of wealth, and men cannot expect to choose those forms of wealth of which nature is least productive and receive the same reward as if they chose for consumption those articles supplied most abundantly by nature. Men complain of the niggardliness of nature, when really the only thing wrong is the universal disposition on the part of men to prefer those forms of wealth of which nature is least productive, instead of other commodities of which nature offers a generous supply. As soon as the productive power of men is increased, it is not used to augment their supply of commodities, but to enable them to obtain articles produced by nature less abundantly than those formerly consumed. Meat is demanded instead of vegetable food, wheat-bread instead of rye-bread, while corn is mainly used as animal food or for making whiskey, and tobacco displaces other crops of which the earth is more productive. The same change in the demand for commodities causes silk to be preferred to the more abundant cotton, seal-skin cloaks to be chosen instead of the equally useful ones made from wool; and on all sides could other examples of a like nature be pointed out.

I am well aware that these changes are often looked upon as the best evidence of an advancing civilization, and that this is especially true in England and in America. The Anglo-Saxon race pride themselves on the fact that they reject the greater part of those articles of food which the land cultivated by them can produce. They love a diet composed almost wholly of beef and white bread, and look down with contempt upon the German with his sausage and black bread, the Frenchman with his soup and frogs, and all other nations that have a diet more in harmony with the natural conditions by which they are surrounded.

It is not my purpose to endeavor to determine which

of these races has the most resources for happiness. However instructive such a study may be, as an economist I am more interested in studying what are the effects of these different modes of the consumption of wealth on its production and distribution. We can choose any form of consumption, but we cannot avoid the necessary effects which accompany our choice. Every soil is more productive of some one crop than of another, and the same soil will produce more when used for a variety of crops than when one only is raised. The land of any country can produce a certain quantity of each kind of food more advantageously than if a greater or less quantity were demanded for consumption. When all the land is put to its most productive use, there is a fixed relation between the quantities of the various articles produced, and if more or less of any article is produced than its proportional share, the gross produce of the whole country will be diminished.

We have, then, two distinct types of civilizations,— the one in which those things are desired of which nature is least productive, the other in which each individual conforms to those external conditions necessary for the greatest possible production. I desire to point out that the economic laws of these two different civilizations are not the same, and that the doctrines whose universality is asserted by the English school of economists are only true of a civilization where the mass of the people prefer those commodities which can be produced by nature only in relatively small quantities. It is only when the land is used to produce a very few articles of food that the Ricardian theory of rent is true, and it is only in those nations desiring but a small variety of food and having but few sources of pleasure where the tendency to increase of population is so great as to be injurious. Under these conditions the gross and average return for labor is so small that a low class of laborers become a necessity, and they can be utilized only by a large scale of production making the laborers dependent upon their employers and preventing free competition through the combination of the few capitalists who control each industry. As soon as a nation decides the use for which its land shall be employed, it determines for the most part the character of its inhabitants, the scale of its industries, the manner in which its wealth shall be distributed, and the degree in which competition shall be really free.

Just laws for the distribution of wealth cannot compensate for the reduction in the average return for labor necessitated by a choice of those articles of food supplied by nature in but very limited quantities. So long as the present mode of consumption continues, neither the nationalization of land nor even the appropriation of all the means of production can increase the average income to such a degree as to make its possessor comfortable and happy. The losses to the laboring classes occasioned by an unequal distribution of wealth are very small when compared with what is lost through a disregard, on their part, of the conditions by which the food-supply is increased. When they comply with these conditions not only will they obtain all the increase of produce, but they will also set in motion causes which will bring to them the greater part of what is now enjoyed by the other classes. The economic conditions making desirable the nationalization of land and other more socialistic measures are those which also raise rent and bring about such a struggle for food as to reduce wages to a minimum. Nowhere can stronger adherents of the Ricardian doctrines be found than among the socialists, and this is because their conception of natural laws accords with the views of Ricardo. If the doctrines of Ricardo are not universally true, a civilization is possible in which each individual, by complying with the surrounding external conditions, can obtain all that reward which nature offers for labor and abstinence, and when men comply with these conditions they will no longer need the above-mentioned measures to insure a just distribution of wealth.

If the social theory of rent is correct, it is necessary

to explain why there is at the present time such an unequal distribution of wealth, and why wages are low
when they might be high. I shall show that when
two different classes of laborers representing two different civilizations contest in the same society for the
occupation of the field of employment, the power to
survive depends, not on a higher average return for
labor, but on the surplus which can be given as rent,
the class commanding the larger surplus getting possession of the field of employment. That class of laborers
which can pay the highest price for food can deprive
others of the necessary means of support, and hence obtain the victory in the contest. For a higher class of
laborers to displace a lower, they must, in a state of free
competition, be able to pay more for food and still have
sufficient incomes remaining to maintain that standard of life to which they are accustomed. When this
cannot be done, the intelligence and skill of the laborers
are reduced, progress and the increase of population are
checked, and society becomes stationary.

The ultimate cause of the present low return for labor
is not to be found in the niggardliness of nature, but
rather in the combination of cheap labor and low interest, by which the price of food is forced so high, and
the value of other commodities so low, that the more
intelligent classes are driven from the field of employment, or their numbers so reduced that they only do

work with which cheap labor cannot compete. So long as nine-tenths of the labor of any society can be performed by a very low class of laborers, as is the case in our present industrial state, the mass of the people will remain ignorant and degraded, unless society by its laws and customs prevents the success of that combination which is the chief cause of our present evils. A higher social state cannot be attained while free competition results merely in a displacement of the higher classes by their inferiors, who, having no desire for, or appreciation of, better things, can force the price of food so high that no one else can compete with them.

In the first chapters of this work the problems relating to land, population, and the effect of increased production on the average return for labor are discussed; and then free competition, the causes of an unequal distribution of wealth, and the hinderances to social progress are considered, and some of the means of bettering our present social state are pointed out.

THE PREMISES

OF

POLITICAL ECONOMY.

CHAPTER I.

RENT.

THE theory of rent as commonly taught makes differences of soil the cause of rent. As some soils are more fertile than others, the produce is raised at different costs of production, so that if the price of the produce is high enough to give the usual profit on that portion of the whole crop which is raised at greatest expense, it will give more than the ordinary profit to those portions raised at less expense. There will therefore be a surplus value in the proceeds from some lands beyond what will cover the expenses and profits of the crops, and the amount of this surplus is said by Ricardo to be the amount of the rent.

There can be no doubt that soils of different degrees

of fertility are in cultivation, but whether this fact is the sole, or even a necessary, condition of rent may well be questioned.

That the poorest land in cultivation should pay no rent requires that there should be no other purpose than cultivation to which the land can be put. This is rarely or never true, as man does not subsist alone on cultivated plants, such as wheat, oats, and corn, but also on plants that require no cultivation, and on animals that can live on uncultivated land; he also has use for lumber and fuel, and the trees from which they are obtained grow on untilled land. When land is needed for cultivation it cannot be had for nothing, since it is valuable to its owners for other purposes. Upon uncultivated land, for instance, cattle and sheep can be kept. Persons who wish to cultivate land must compete with those who wish the land for grazing purposes, and as all lands that can be cultivated can be used for pasture, and will yield the usual profit and leave something for rent, those who wish to till the land must be able to bid over the herders in their offers of rent. The same is true in regard to timber land. Trees will grow in sufficient quantities on all land which can be cultivated more than to repay for the labor and capital needed to prepare them for market, and all tillable timber lands will yield a rent to their owners. Hence persons who desire to obtain this land for tilling must pay more rent than the owners can obtain from those who cut wood.

The rent of uncultivated land does not, as does that of cultivated land, depend upon the differences of fertility. Cultivated land, whether good or poor, must be ploughed and worked just the same, the poor, if there is a difference, needing more labor than the good. Hence the cost of cultivation is by the acre, while the profit is according to fertility. If two persons raise equal amounts of produce, one from one hundred acres, the other from two hundred acres of land, he who works the two hundred acres should pay a much lower rent than the other, since he must retain a double amount to repay him for his extra cost of cultivation. But in grazing the case is different. If two hundred acres of a certain land will keep as many sheep or cattle as one hundred acres of better land, the two hundred acres of poor land will rent for as much as the one hundred acres of good land. The renter of the two hundred acres, having no additional expenses, is at no disadvantage in competing with the renter of the one hundred acres, and must pay as much rent. The same is true of timber land. It costs no more to cut a quantity of wood from poor than from good land. The rent of timber lands will therefore be proportional to the timber on the lands, and rent can be paid for the poor as well as for the good.

There are still other purposes for which land can be used profitably. On very sterile lands, for instance, wild game will thrive, which will more than repay the cost of killing and bringing to market; and as such game is often killed merely for sport, poor lands are in some countries, especially in England, set apart solely for hunting preserves. The rich men who own these preserves may pay more for sport than their game would fetch in market, but that such lands would yield a rent if the owners wish it is shown by the fact that men violate law and kill game in these preserves, even at great risk. There would certainly be no poachers if the value of the game did not exceed the cost of killing it.

It is often asserted that there is land so distant from market that it can yield no rent. In new countries this may sometimes be the case, but distance from market will not of itself remain a permanent reason why any land cannot pay rent. A land-owner has a choice of local and distant markets, and no produce will be sent to a distant market unless the price there is enough higher than the price at home to pay cost of transportation. This additional price can usually be paid, since production on a large scale at distant places is much more productive than local industries on a small scale. Producers on a small scale can, however, offer a price for food high enough to yield the landlord a considerable rent, and more than this rent must be offered by distant producers before they can displace local industries.

In view of these facts, it is clear that all cultivated lands, except in very new countries, must pay rent. Even the poorest land cultivated must pay rent, for those wishing it must compete with those who want it for purposes not requiring cultivation.

The Ricardian theory of rent supposes that the greatest return is to be obtained when all the land of a country is cultivated. This, however, is not true, since from all the land of a country less produce will be obtained than if only a part is cultivated. To have a proper rainfall, it is necessary that a large part of the land of a country should be covered with trees, and if these are cut away to bring all the land into cultivation, while the owners of the forest lands may profit by it, the owners of the other lands will lose more than the first gain, and on the whole the country will lose, since, the gross production being diminished, a less population than before can be supported. When the greater part of a country is cultivated, the way to support a larger population is not through increasing the area under cultivation, for this will lessen the gross return, but through improving that already under cultivation.

The effect on the gross return of the country of tilling poor lands instead of using them for forestry, is clearly shown by the floods on the Ohio and Mississippi Rivers. At the sources of these rivers the forests are being cleared away so that the ground may be cultivated. The waters of these rivers are precipitated so rapidly into the valleys below that they are overflowed, and much of the best land in the country rendered useless for cultivation. If the poorer lands on the mountain-sides are cleared and cultivated the valley lands cannot be, since they will be subject to overflow. As a result there will be a movement of population from the fertile valleys to the sterile hill and mountain-sides, and a reduction of the gross production of the country. A country can till either the fertile valleys or the sterile mountain-sides, but not both.

Clearly, then, the fact that there are untilled lands in a country does not prove that there are lands in cultivation which yield no rent, for the produce of a country will be greater when certain lands are not cultivated but are covered with forests. It is said that one-fourth of the land of a country should be in forests. Although this proportion may be too large, yet the question of importance is not what is the relative fertility of the worst and best lands in a country, but what is the fertility of the better lands that remain after a proper portion is reserved for forests, since the poorest lands can be used for producing trees, and the best reserved for cultivation.

The most important objection to the Ricardian theory

of rent is that lands do not remain in the same ratio
of fertility as that in which they are regarded when
they are first brought into cultivation. Ricardo talks
of the inexhaustible qualities of the soil, and later
writers, though qualifying his statements somewhat,
still hold them in the main. All soils vary with time
in their fertility; bad lands become good by proper
treatment, and poor usage ruins the best of lands.
Hence lands tend strongly to an equality when once
brought into cultivation; the rich lands lose most in
fertility under improper tillage, while the poor lands
gain most under proper tillage. When lands are badly
cultivated, much more strength is taken from the good
lands than from the poor, and they will therefore lose
their fertility more rapidly. If wheat is raised on
three grades of land yielding respectively ten, twenty,
and thirty bushels per acre, and if nothing is done to
replace the lost qualities, the best lands will decrease in
fertility more rapidly than the others, since more is
taken from the soil. By the time the capacity of the
poorest land is reduced to nine bushels per acre, that
of the better lands will be reduced to something like
eighteen and twenty-seven bushels, and under continu-
ous cultivation without manures the productivity of the
lands would finally be on a par with that of the poor;
all lands thus handled would become equally poor, and
rent from differences of soil would cease.

On the other hand, if lands are properly cultivated, the poor lands will increase in fertility more rapidly than the rich. I have shown that if nothing is returned to the land it will soon become worthless through exhaustion. When lands are properly cultivated a return is made, but this return is made to the land from which it was taken. If one field yields twenty bushels an acre and another thirty bushels, a farmer will not put three loads of manure on the good field to two on the poor field, but will place most of the manure, if not all, for a time at least, on the poor field, which will gradually yield more proportionally, and the difference in rent between the two fields will gradually lessen, and probably at length entirely cease.

Variations in the rate of interest or wages change the value of lands. We call at present land in Kansas poor in comparison with land in New York, but this is not because the same labor will not produce as much in Kansas as in New York, but because interest and wages are higher in Kansas, so that land of equal fertility in the two States will not yield the same rent. But when interest and wages in Kansas fall to their level in New York, the land of both States will be classed as good, and the differences of rent will cease or at least decrease.

The distribution of population also affects our estimation of the value of land. When a country is new, sparsely settled, and distant from a market, lands of

great fertility will be classed as poor which a few generations later, when the population has much increased,
will be regarded as very good, and yield a large rent.

In like manner a reduced cost of transportation
alters our estimation of the value of land, causing us
now to regard lands as good which a few years ago
were classed as non-rent-producing. For these and
similar reasons the proportion of the land on the earth
regarded as poor is constantly decreasing.

Ricardo and his school always speak of wheat lands,
barley lands, pasture lands, etc., as if each field was good
for one crop alone, and would be most profitable to its
owner only when used in the cultivation of this particular crop. Nothing can be more false than this view of
the case. If any field is used to grow one crop only,
it will decrease in fertility and soon yield little or no
rent. Nothing in agriculture is better established than
the necessity of a rotation of crops to prevent a loss of
fertility. For this reason the value of land cannot be
estimated by what it will produce of any one crop.
An average must be struck from all the crops which
must be raised to obtain the proper rotation. The
fact that of a particular crop a piece of land will yield
no more than enough to pay the cost of cultivation
does not show that no rent can be paid for such land.
Let us suppose that for a certain field, wheat, corn,
grass, and pasture would give a proper rotation of

3*

crops. If a follower of Ricardo should pass by the field when sown to wheat, he would see some poor spots, and say that there is land which yields no rent. The next year he would see poor spots likewise in the corn crop, and on the following years in the land when used for a meadow and pasture, and from this would assert that although the farmer paid rent for all the land the rent of some of it was only nominal, and that here accordingly was a margin of cultivation which yielded no rent. A careful examination would reveal that the poor spots in the wheat were not those in the meadow; that where no corn grew there was splendid pasture; that in dry years the poor spots are here, in wet years there; in short, that in a series of years every part may be in turn regarded as good and bad, and that the farmer can afford to pay rent for all, since some time during the series of years each part will make more than a return for labor and capital expended upon it.

The plausibility of the Ricardian theory arises from the temporary circumstances attending the extension of cultivation. In this country, first it was New York that was on the margin of cultivation, then it was Ohio, then Illinois, and now it is Kansas and Nebraska; soon it will be Montana and other far-off territories. But none of these places stay at the margin of cultivation, and soon rent makes its appearance, and will in time become as high as in the oldest States.

None of the differences which tend to augment rent are of a permanent character; they are, on the contrary, of a very changeable nature. The order in which the lands were brought into cultivation affords no clue as to our present estimation of them. It may be granted that when we are obliged to extend the area of cultivation we always take what we regard the best of the uncultivated lands; but when these lands are once cultivated for a series of years we cannot say they yield no rent because they were last brought into cultivation. Our estimation of their value has most probably changed in the mean time. If a country is in a progressive state, all these differences of fertility will diminish, and probably in time cease; all land increasing in fertility under better conditions, the poorer ones, however, more rapidly, being most susceptible of improvement.

As I have stated before, I do not deny all the assumptions of the current theory of rent. I dispute only the one which claims that the price of the whole crop is determined by the cost of producing that portion raised at the greatest expense. The proof of this proposition is often presented in the following manner: If the price of produce was not sufficient to cover this cost with ordinary profit there would be no inducement for farmers to continue the production of this the most costly portion of the crop, and a farmer will not continue to produce at a loss; on the other hand, if the price was more than sufficient to give the ordinary rate of profit new lands would be brought into cultivation, until the price of produce would be reduced to the cost of producing the most costly part. In this argument there is a fact of great importance overlooked which, when rightly considered, will change the whole view of the case. There is much labor to be performed before land can be cultivated. The land must be cleared of timber, it must be drained, stones and other obstructions must be removed, and, lastly, the land must be ploughed and the ground prepared before a crop can be raised. If these facts were not true, if the new land could be cultivated with no more trouble than the old lands can be changed from one crop to another, then we might be able to predict that the poorest land would go out of cultivation when the price of produce fell, and that more would be cultivated when the price rose. But nothing of the sort can be predicted. When new land is brought into cultivation the price must be high enough to remunerate satisfactorily those preparing the land for tillage, besides paying the cost of cultivating the crop; but the land being once tillable, it will not cease to be used so long as the price of produce will repay the cost of cultivation alone. What has been expended in bringing the land into cultivation cannot be withdrawn, nor will the land be withdrawn from cultivation because no return is obtained for this expenditure.

Let us consider carefully the difference between these two elements, the one necessary to bring land into cultivation, the other to keep it there. If three thousand dollars must be expended to prepare a given farm for cultivation, and two thousand dollars and the labor of two men are required to cultivate it, then the farm will not be brought into cultivation until the price of produce will be sufficient to pay the wages of two men and the interest on five thousand dollars; but when the land is once cultivated, it will not be withdrawn so long as the price of produce is sufficient to pay the wages of the two laborers and the interest on two thousand dollars. In other words, there might be a fall in price of produce equal to the interest on three thousand dollars without a reduction in the quantity of food produced. When lands have been once cleared of timber and brought into a proper state for cultivation that work is done once for all, and the capital and labor so expended become intermingled with the natural qualities of the soil. The revenue which the owner receives for such expenditure is properly to be regarded as rent, for it is governed by the laws of rent. Whether or no, return can be obtained for capital thus expended must depend on the causes which determine rent, and not on those which determine interest; and

c

the fact that no return is obtained for money once expended has no tendency to reduce the amount of production. But with the circulating capital used on the farm the case is different: if no return is obtained it will be withdrawn and cultivation cease. Buildings, fences, etc., when once made, do not last forever, but must constantly be renewed, and if the price of produce falls so that the ordinary profit is not obtained on this capital, it will gradually be withdrawn and production will be in this way checked or reduced.

It is clear, therefore, that the laws which regulate the bringing of new lands into cultivation, and those according to which land will be withdrawn from cultivation, are very different, and that there is a large margin within which the price of produce may vary without a change in the quantity produced. Economists usually confuse two very different things in their arguments on this point. When they say that a capitalist will not bring new lands into cultivation unless the price of produce is sufficient to pay the cost of production, under this cost is included not only the cost of the labor necessary to cultivate the land, but also enough more to repay him for the cost of preparing the land. When, however, they say, if the price of produce is not sufficient to repay the cost of production land will be withdrawn from cultivation, the term cost of production must be understood to exclude the cost of bringing the land into cultivation, and to include only a remuneration for the labor expended and interest for the circulating capital. Let us suppose that sixty cents a bushel as the price of wheat suffices to repay the cost of production,—in other words, that such a price will properly remunerate labor and provide the interest on the circulating capital,—and that twenty cents on each bushel is needed to pay the interest on the capital expended in bringing the land into cultivation. Then the price of wheat must rise to eighty cents before new land will be brought into cultivation, but must fall below sixty cents before any land will be withdrawn. No changes in price between these figures, sixty and eighty cents, will affect the quantity of wheat produced.

If we keep these facts in mind we will see how faulty are the arguments supporting the doctrine that the price of the whole crop is determined by the cost of producing that portion which is produced at the greatest expense. There is always a large margin between the price which will remunerate those who bring new land into cultivation and that which will cause land to be withdrawn from cultivation. This margin is larger in old countries than in new ones, as those lands to the cultivation of which the obstructions are the least, which require the least clearing, draining, etc., will be the first cultivated, the subsequent additions being necessarily made from lands more difficult of preparation. Prairie land will be cultivated before wooded lands, high and dry lands before low and wet, lands naturally rich before those which require manures to render them tillable. As the demand for food increases the price of produce necessary to cause new lands to be cultivated increases, but the price which must be paid to prevent land from being thrown out of cultivation tends to become lower than before, since every improvement lessens the cost of production on all the cultivated land. Thus if in a new country sixty cents for wheat be the lowest limit of possible fluctuation at that time and eighty cents the upper limit, as the country grows older and the demand for food increases the upper limit will rapidly rise to one dollar, one dollar and twenty cents, one dollar and forty cents, and so on, while the lower limit will probably, through improved cultivation, slowly decline to fifty-nine cents, fifty-eight cents, and still lower figures. For this reason, as the demand for food increases the farther will its price be from the cost of cultivating the poorest land that has been prepared for tillage, and a knowledge of this cost will not enable us to determine what is the rent of the better grades of land.

The increase of the margin of fluctuation of values as the land of a country is gradually brought into use, causes the price of food to change more rapidly and

to a greater amount than where only the easily cultivated land is in use. If the supply of food exceeds
the demand, the price falls below the lower limit before
the supply will be reduced. On the other hand, a slight
deficiency of the supply will force the price above the
upper limit, since there will be no increase in the
amount of land cultivated until this limit is reached.
Mineral products, following the same law that agricultural produce does, show much more clearly the effect
of the increase of the margin of fluctuation. The
mines which are easily opened and prepared for use
are first worked, and those having greater obstructions
are resorted to when more mineral products are desired. An increased demand for mineral products
causes so high a price that new mines with great obstacles to their use must be opened, but once in use
these mines can be worked at so low a cost that the
supply of mineral products will be reduced only after
a great fall in their price.

Gold and silver, being minerals, must also in time
lose that firmness of value which has thus far made
them so valuable as money. The supply from sources
having but few obstructions either is, or soon will be,
exhausted, and resort must be had to mines requiring
much labor to open them up. The effect on the value
of silver of the opening up of costly mines has been
very marked during the last few years. From the

present low price of silver, however, we cannot justly infer that the permanent cost of production has been reduced. The supply of silver has exceeded the demand, and as there are no mines in use which have a high cost of production, a great decline of price was a necessary consequence. When the mines now in use are exhausted the price will probably rise above its former price, with a liability of another great fall in value when new mines are brought into use.

During modern times the rapid increase in the demand for food has kept its price steadily at the upper limit. There are, however, at the present time many indications that this will not be true in the future. We are probably nearing a period when the changes in the value of food will be as rapid, and to as great an amount, as is now the case with mineral products. A slight change in the relation of the supply to the demand will occasion a great change in the value of food wherever there is but little or no land at the margin of cultivation, which will be withdrawn from use when the price begins to fall.

In opposition to the theory of Ricardo I offer the following, which will, I think, be found more in harmony with all the facts. Lands vary chiefly in two ways, in fertility and in the amount of obstructions necessary to be removed in order that they may be cultivated. Under obstructions are classed all hinderances which, when once removed, do not require a continual outlay of capital and labor to keep the land fit for cultivation. All land must be drained, and most of it must be cleared of timber and stones, and other like expenses must be incurred. When, however, this is once done, no outlay of capital and labor is needful beyond the regular expense of cultivation. When a country is first settled the lands least obstructed are first cultivated, as the population increases, and new lands with greater obstructions to cultivation must be tilled, the price of produce must rise, since no one will bring any land into cultivation unless the price of produce is sufficient not only to repay the annual cost of cultivation, but also to give him the interest on the money laid out in subduing the land. Every increase in the demand for food requires the cultivation of more land, and this cannot be done until the price rises enough to repay the cost of bringing in new lands. This cost is constantly increasing, the least obstructed lands naturally being brought first into cultivation.

Besides the obstructions to the cultivation of land there are differences of fertility, but these are very limited in their nature and would not alone ever cause a very large rise in the price of produce. Fields sloping to the north are not so fertile as those sloping to the south, upland is not so fertile as valleys, in some places clay land may not be as good as sandy land, and in other places sandy land is inferior to clay, and so through all the categories of difference. In a very early stage of the growth of a country all these kinds of land were cultivated, and when afterwards new land is brought into cultivation, the obstructions having been removed, it falls into a class of lands already cultivated, and has no greater annual cost of cultivation than other lands of the same class previously tilled.

As is well known, Mr. Carey contends that the course of cultivation is always from the thin high lands to the rich bottom-lands, which cannot be at first cultivated by reason of their unhealthfulness and of the great and prolonged labor necessary for clearing and draining them. Whether this is always true, or true often enough to be regarded the general rule, is a matter of no moment to my position. What I contend is that at a time when the price of food was low our ancestors did cultivate as poor lands as any that are now left uncultivated, and that therefore, if the price should again fall to what it then was, poor lands would not go out of cultivation. That our ancestors cultivated high and thin land on the hills John Stuart Mill does not attempt to deny, but he asserts that at the present time in all old countries, as England and France, all, or nearly all, the fertile lands are cultivated, and that the extension of cultivation is from the plains to the hills. This is doubtless true, but it must be remembered also that some of the lands on these same hills are already cultivated and have been for centuries, and that the lands yet untilled when once prepared for cultivation are no poorer than those first cultivated, the extension of cultivation having been from the hills to the valleys, and then back to the hills. Why the hills should be first cultivated is very apparent. The hills afforded better means of defence, they were healthier, and from the stand-point of our ancestors, obstructions to cultivation were there the least. These were all important facts to our fore-fathers, who had many enemies, poor tools, and few means of resisting disease.

However, in the course of time, when our ancestors had obtained more knowledge and had the requisite security through improved government, they settled in the valleys and obtained a better return for their labor on the more fertile lands. But when they cultivated the valleys, why were not the less productive hill-sides abandoned? There can be but one reply. The per-manent cost of production must have been a low one. The labor which had been expended to bring them into cultivation was permanently fixed and could not be withdrawn. The lands continued to be cultivated be-cause a return was obtained on the labor and capital annually expended on them, but no new lands of this

4*

class could be brought into cultivation so long as some of the more fertile valleys were unused. When the valley lands were all cultivated, and more food was needed on account of increased population, the price of food rose, so that it became profitable to cultivate new lands on the hills. In other words, the price of food was high enough to pay the annual cost of production and leave enough to pay the interest on the money expended to bring the lands into cultivation. It must not be forgotten, however, that hill lands have been in cultivation for centuries, and these new lands will have no greater annual cost of cultivation than those formerly tilled have, and this cost must be a low one, as they were cultivated when the price of food was at the lowest point of which we have any knowledge.

All circumstances, whatever they be, which prevent new lands from being cultivated, but are no longer operative when lands are once in cultivation, I term obstacles to the extension of cultivation, and it is to these, and not to differences of fertility, to which the constantly-increasing price of food must be attributed.

I will now present in summary the facts which show the defects of the current theory of rent.

First. To obtain uncultivated land for tillage, farmers must compete with those who can afford to pay rent for uncultivated land by using it for pasture, for wood, and many other similar purposes. For this reason the poorest land in cultivation must pay rent, since, if the farmers would not pay rent, the landlords would let it to herders and others who could afford to give much for the use of uncultivated land.

Second. The greatest return is not obtained when all the land of a country is cultivated. There is great need of forests to secure a proper rainfall, and hence the question is not what is the difference between the best land of a country and the poorest, but what is the difference in the soils after the poorest are set aside for forests, poor lands being as useful for forests as the good. When the proper amount of land is reserved there can be no doubt but that the remainder is fertile enough to yield a considerable rent.

Third. The disadvantages of an unfavorable situation alone can never cause any land to pay no rent. Home industries on a small scale are always productive enough to offer a price for food sufficient to yield considerable rent, and more than this price must be obtained before food will be sent to distant markets.

Fourth. The fertility of land is not a fixed quantity, but by poor culture all lands soon become equally poor, while with a proper culture all lands improve rapidly, and even the poorest are soon fertile enough to pay a large rent.

Fifth. The mass of the so-called poor lands do not lack fertility, but are rated poor because in our present estimation their situation is unfavorable, because interest and wages are high, or the cost of transportation is great, and for other reasons which affect their present desirableness. Most, if not all, of these circumstances have their cause in the present distribution of population, and as population in the vicinity of these lands increases they will yield a large rent and be classed as good lands.

Sixth. There are many obstructions to cultivation which must be removed. While the price of produce must be high enough to remunerate the capitalists who remove them and prepare the ground for cultivation, when they are once removed, the price of produce may fall, and yet these lands will not be withdrawn from cultivation.

Each of these facts shows plainly the defects of the Ricardian theory of rent, but when we consider them together they display much more glaringly the deficiencies of this theory, which attributes all rent to the original differences of soils. The original fertility of the soil is an element of but little relative importance, since the obstacles which retard the cultivation of inferior lands are no longer in operation when these lands are once brought into use.

One important problem in the discussion of rent I have purposely omitted. Does the demand for commodities, and the kind and variety of the food consumed, affect rent by changing our estimate of the relative value of lands differing in soil and climate? No solution of the rent question can be had without a consideration of this important problem, but as the points involved are remote from those treated in the foregoing discussion, I will consider them separately in the following chapter.

CHAPTER II.

THE SOCIAL CAUSES PRODUCING A HIGH PRICE OF FOOD.

THUS far only the physical capacities of the earth to produce food, and the conditions on which increased quantities of food can be obtained, have been examined. Now I wish to call attention to the importance of the reaction of the consumption on the production of wealth, and to the influence which the economy of the food-supply exerts on production. The current theory is that consumption has no influence on production, and that a demand for commodities is not a demand for labor. It determines merely the direction of labor, but not the quantity or efficiency of the labor, or the total aggregate of wealth produced. This proposition is set down by most economists as one of the most fundamental and best established doctrines of Political Economy. This subject, like many others in Political Economy, is much obscured by the nature of the attack to which the current doctrine has been subjected, by which the attention of economists has been diverted from the real issue involved to questions almost frivolous. It is against the popular notion that the extravagance of the rich is a blessing to the poor, by giving them employment, that the arguments of economists have been directed, and in so doing they have laid down propositions which, while strong enough to withstand the opposition met with on popular grounds, are very weak when examined from another and more reasonable point of view.

I shall first show the influence which changes in the demand for commodities have on the aggregate production whenever the change is from a commodity which nature can produce less abundantly to one capable of being produced more abundantly. Of some commodities nature can produce more than of others, and if the more abundant are demanded a greater population can be supported, and for their labor a greater proportional return can be had, than if something yielded by nature less abundantly was demanded. On a given area more rye can be obtained for the same labor than wheat, and more corn and potatoes than rye, and in many climates more rice than corn or potatoes. Hence if corn or potatoes are demanded for food instead of rice, a much smaller population can be supported, and a still smaller if rye is wanted, while wheat will support the smallest population of all. But this is not all, for by examining the laws of nature more closely we shall find that the abundance in which nature can produce given articles varies with the changes of climate and soil. Some climates and soils are naturally adapted to wheat, some to oats, others to rye, barley, or potatoes, and still others to rice, sugar, and other tropical products, while other parts are best fitted for the pasture of cattle. If this is true, a change in the demand for food, from commodities of which under the circumstances nature can produce but small quantities to those which can be produced in greater abundance, will increase both the gross and average return for labor, and at the same time bring about a more equal distribution of wealth. Let us suppose the demand for wheat has been so great as to cause not only all natural wheat lands to be sown to wheat, but also some of the potato lands. This would not only cause a much greater proportional expenditure of labor than if a less quantity of wheat was demanded, but also a great increase of rent on the good wheat lands, all of which would come out of the consumers' revenue. If the demand for food should change so that less wheat and more potatoes were wanted, the price of wheat would fall, the demand being supplied from a better class of wheat land than before, while the price of potatoes would not rise, or at least not rise as much as the price of wheat fell. The community then would have a double gain, less labor would be required to supply its demand for food, and rent would fall; lands poor in their capacity to produce wheat being no longer cultivated for wheat but for potatoes, for which they are especially adapted.

Ricardo, in discussing the causes of rent, views the whole world as used for the production of a single article, and because any one article cannot be raised on all soils and in every climate at an equal cost of labor, he grades all land according to its power of producing some one article, and then shows that rent will rise as lands less fitted for the production of this article are used for its production. Certainly if the people demand only wheat, for instance, as food, they must pay a high rent; but this does not prove that an increase of population necessitates a rise of rent. Suppose there are four classes of land, of which the first is best adapted for wheat, the second for rye, the third for corn, and the fourth for potatoes. If only one article were in demand, so that all the four classes of land must be used for its production, every extension of cultivation would be accompanied by a rise in the price of food. On the other hand, if all of these articles were desired, and the demand for each article was in proportion to the land best fitted for its production, there would be no rent from differences in fertility, or at least much less rent than if only one article were produced. The rise of rent merely shows that there is too much of some one kind of food demanded, and does not prove that more food cannot be obtained without increasing the cost of production.

Besides the difference of climate and soil, the rotation of crops has a great effect on the quantity produced, and to have a proper rotation there must be a demand for all the products required for the rotation; and a change in the demand for commodities which allows a better rotation of crops causes a much greater quantity of food to be obtained with no greater expenditure of labor.

If nature produces some articles of food more abundantly than others, and some articles grow more advantageously in one climate or soil than in others, and if any soil will produce a variety of articles by a rotation of crops in greater abundance than one article, the population which a country can support cannot be determined without a knowledge of what the inhabtants will demand for food. A much greater population can be provided with subsistence if they demand for food what nature can produce most abundantly than if they demand something of which nature can supply but a very limited quantity. So much has this fact been misunderstood that many economists have maintained that those nations prospered best who used the most expensive food. The use of wheat and beef is regarded as indications of a high standard of life, while the use of potatoes and rice is looked upon as the

cause of the misery and degradation of the countries
which use them as the chief articles of diet. There is
a seeming justification of this view in the conditions
of those countries which use a cheap and abundant
kind of food. India, Egypt, and Ireland, where potatoes, rice, and other like articles of food are used,
have a much lower standard of life than England,
where wheat, beef, and other food-stuffs, which cannot
be supplied by nature except in more limited quantities, are demanded. Wherever the tendencies producing an unequal distribution of wealth are strong
there can be no doubt that a nation runs a great
danger in the introduction of a cheap article of food,
since by the use of such a food the probabilities of
increasing the effects of the unequal distribution are
much augmented. So long as a dear kind of food is
used, those of the laborers who wish to better their
condition can, by using a cheaper food themselves, obtain a great advantage, which will aid them much towards their improvement; if, however, all the laborers
use the cheaper food, those desiring to save have no
advantage, and are thus practically without hope of
improvement, and all remain in a low and degraded
state, while the few to whom the benefit of an unequal
distribution comes enjoy all the produce of the industry of the people. On the other hand, if there
is no danger of an unequal distribution, or if a nation

adopt proper means to overcome the tendencies in this direction, the advantages of cheap food are very apparent, as a much greater population can be supported with a much less expenditure of labor than when only dear food is used.

The use of cheap food must not be confounded with the use of a single article, such as potatoes or rice, for a diet; for the laws of nature are so arranged that a mixed diet is always the cheapest. For a time land will produce one article, such as potatoes or wheat, very abundantly, but the fertility will soon decrease unless the crop is changed and some other article is raised, since only by a proper rotation of crops can the fertility of the soil be maintained or increased. So, too, as climates and soils are different, nations can supply their wants by exchange, and get many articles of food with less labor than if they attempted to raise them at home. The cheapest food then will contain all the variety necessary to support life, and will be in harmony with the tastes and inclinations of all who are willing to adjust themselves to the natural conditions by which the gross and average return for labor is increased.

Even when the amount of the food-supply is known the number of the population which it supports cannot be determined, unless it is also known what commodities this population will demand. Some commodities are

richer in food-material than others, and the consumption
of these will create a larger demand for land than the
consumption of the others, and if such articles be used,
only a much smaller population can be supported. It
is usually regarded as axiomatic by economists that
each person requires a fixed quantity of food, and when
the food-supply is known the amount of the population
can be inferred; but this is not true. Food is not only
used to support life, but is also largely consumed for
the mere pleasure which the consumption gives, so that
almost every one, if he has the means, consumes two or
three times as much as is needed for the preservation of
life and health. Wherever this is done not only is the
population much reduced, but also the sum of the pleasures to be obtained by each one is greatly diminished,
since other pleasures of a different kind are lost when
the food is consumed instead of being converted, as it
may be, into other kinds of enjoyment. The pleasure
derived from food is exclusive, and is only enjoyed
by the person who consumes the food, while many
other pleasures can be enjoyed by a great number without any more expenditure of labor than if they were
produced for the pleasure of one person. The different
sources of enjoyment presented by a pleasant dinner
illustrate clearly the various degrees of exclusiveness
which different pleasures possess. The floral decora-
tions, the table furniture, and the tasteful preparation

of the food can be enjoyed by all alike. These pleasures do not depend on the amount of food as do the pleasures procured by consuming the edible dishes. The latter pleasures are exclusive and demand an increase of food for each additional person enjoying it.

Compare, again, the pleasure derived from beer and music. For each additional glass of beer additional labor is required, and if a double quantity is demanded, twice the amount of labor is needed in general to produce it. This increase of expense is not true of music, since a large number of persons can be entertained with music by an orchestra with no more labor than if the number was small. That one enjoys the music does not debar another from a like enjoyment, but the enjoyment of both is rather increased by the fact that they have a common pleasure. The same lack of exclusiveness in consumption is true of books,—a book that would exchange for twenty glasses of beer can be enjoyed in turn by a thousand people, while, if the beer had been purchased instead of the book, but twenty of the thousand would have had any enjoyment, and the rest would have been excluded. Art is also similar to music and books in the amount of pleasure that can be derived from a small expenditure of labor and of the food-supply. So many persons cannot enjoy a painting simultaneously as can enjoy a piece of music, but as the painting lasts for a long time while the music does not, the painting is in time capable of giving as much pleasure at as little cost as can be obtained by any other means.

The examples which have been given lie at the extremes in regard to labor and the consumption of food necessary to produce a given amount of pleasure. Beer and other articles of like character require the greatest amount of labor and consumption of food, while music, books, and art require the least, in proportion to the amount of pleasure obtained. Between these extremes are innumerable other commodities, some requiring more and others less labor and consumption of food in their production, and thus they approximate one or the other of the class of commodities above mentioned.

The number of acres required to produce the food and liquor of each person determines the population of any section and the demand for labor. If the average person requires twenty acres to produce what he eats and drinks, there is but one-half the demand for labor that there would be if he consumed only the produce of ten acres and exchanged the produce of the other ten acres with artisans for other commodities. This fact can be well illustrated by taking many parts of the South, where every farmer has a still to make his own liquor, and raises his own tobacco and corn, but has little or no exchange with the outside world.

Suppose in such a society there should be a change of demand from liquor and tobacco to clothes. This demand for cloth would cause an increased demand for labor. All the labor formerly employed to produce the tobacco, and grain for liquor, would now be employed in raising food for the cloth-makers, while more cloth must be made to supply the increased demand. If now the people desired good houses, and reduced their consumption of food in the form of liquor and tobacco still more, they would permit the population to increase, and the additional laborers could find employment in building houses.

There is another important circumstance affecting the consumption of food in the degree of exclusiveness of family life. Where each family lives in seclusion, having a private house, preparing its own food, and doing all other work without any co-operation, the consumption of the food-supply is many times greater than it would be if the same families should so live as to allow the proper degree of division of labor. Certainly in the cooking and serving of food alone at least half of it is wasted or rendered worthless by the inefficiency of the labor employed in private life. It is a necessary disadvantage of private life that the labor be unskilled, as no person can wash, cook, and perform all the other work of a family with as little waste and as efficiently as the labor could be performed under conditions where each person is engaged in one occupation only. Where bread is made in a bakery, the same material will make much more bread and of a better quality than where each family bakes for itself. For example, take the difference in this respect between America and Germany. In Germany all bread is made in a bakery, while in America most of it is baked at home. It is no exaggeration to say that German rye-bread is more palatable than the wheat-bread served up on the ordinary American table. It is only when furnished with the finest qualities of wheat-flour that the ordinary cook can produce edible bread, while a baker can produce a better article with the poorest of wheat. The same waste is true of every department of private life, and when the present mode of living becomes modified so as to allow a greater division of labor, there will be an important economy of the food-supply, and a much larger population will be provided with subsistence without an increase of cost.

The amount of labor that can be employed in a country depends on the economy of the food-supply, and any change in consumption from commodities which draw largely on the food-supply to those requiring less land for their production, creates a demand for additional labor, and allows for an increase of population. So also a change in the demand from commodities which give only brief pleasure to those giving pleasure for a longer time, or to more persons at one time, will increase the demand for labor and the gross amount of pleasures to be enjoyed by the people. Clothes last for enjoyment a longer time than tobacco. A change of demand from tobacco to clothes will not only increase the demand for labor, but also the amount of pleasure to be enjoyed, since by the additional labor more is produced, and what is produced gives pleasure for a longer time than the former product. In the same way a demand for beautiful houses instead of fine clothes adds to the amount of the pleasures which any community has to enjoy, since houses last longer than clothes, can be enjoyed by many at the same time, and do not draw so largely on the food-supply, while public parks, museums, libraries, and musical concerts encroach still less on the food-supply, as they are most permanent in their effects, and the enjoyment of them by one person does not exclude the enjoyment of them by others.

As each individual demands commodities that will require the use of additional land for their production, or as he consumes his wealth in a manner which excludes others from enjoying his wealth with him, the demand for land increases and rent and the price of food rise. An unequal distribution of wealth is the result, and this cause brings about other changes, which increase still further the demand for land and raise the price of food. Rich persons, as a class, do not desire commodities so much for the pleasure which can be derived from them as for the display of their wealth. It is the rareness of an article which makes it desirable to them. Cheap things which all may have are passed by, and commodities are sought after of which there are not enough to supply the wants of every person. This spirit soon pervades all classes, each person desiring articles rarer and more costly than those lower in life can afford to purchase. Fashionable articles are desired and new clothes are purchased before utility demands a change, thus causing a great waste of labor and material. The desire to excel others is also visible in the desire of the rich to have all their amusement in private, although a multitude might have the pleasure without increase of cost. Their libraries, their art collections, their parks, must be their exclusive property, not because their pleasure is thereby increased, but because the possession of such treasures is beyond the means of ordinary people. This desire for rare and costly articles, especially when accompanied by the desire of individuals to have them for their exclusive use, creates a demand for land and raises the price of food. So long as this spirit prevails to as great a degree as at present, the present high price of food will continue; and this spirit must cease before cheap food and an equal distribution of wealth are possible.

The effect of a change of demand from commodities requiring a large consumption of the food-supply to those better economizing it, is as marked on the distribution of wealth as on the production. Let us suppose ten men working together, four of whom produce the food-supply, while six are engaged in making other articles desired for consumption. Each man would have a right to one-tenth of what is produced, and as the amount of food produced is but four-tenths of the gross production, any four of the men could, by taking all their share in food, exhaust the whole supply and leave the other six without food. The knowledge or fear that they would do this would break up the whole social arrangement and cause each one to work by himself, or the price of food would rise and that of other commodities fall until there was no danger that any one would demand more than his share of food. No one could live without food, and every one would give the whole produce of his labor rather than perish; hence if the six engaged in other than agricultural pursuits were determined to exchange what they produced for food alone, they would reduce the value of their produce until the whole produce of each would procure but one-tenth of the food-supply, which is the same amount that they would have received had they in the first place consented to an equitable exchange and not endeavored to obtain only food for their productions, while they have lost the share of one another's production which they would have obtained by a just division.

If each person increases his demand for food, either the number of the people in a country must be reduced, or a greater part of the labor must be devoted to the production of food. In either case there is a decline of civilization, as where nothing but food is produced, however abundant it may be, there is no civilization, and such a society will be low and ignorant. This shows that there is a condition to a high civilization which is nearly always overlooked. A high civilization requires that the labor of each should be exchanged for much more than enough to support the laborer, but he must not endeavor to obtain food in exchange for all his labor. The amount of food for which the labor of each will exchange is the measure of his wages. It shows how many of the laborers can be spared from the production of food to produce other articles. For each laborer, however, to endeavor to obtain food for all his wages would destroy the civilization, or cause such an unequal distribution of wealth that the wages of each would only suffice to purchase the amount of food necessary for existence. If the people in any society do not choose to scatter, and each one raise food for himself, they must content themselves with the food necessary for their support, and each take his

6

share of the other commodities produced, or they will force upon themselves such an unequal distribution of wealth that their wages will furnish them but a bare living. The latter alternative is what most societies take, and as a result wages are at a minimum and the price of food high. Every one endeavors to get more than his share of food, and as there is no way in which the part can be made equal to the whole, they obtain no more than if they had consented to take an equitable share, and at the same time they lose all their share of the other products of labor.

The demand for commodities of which nature can produce but very limited quantities, and the desire for food to be consumed for mere pleasure over and above what is sufficient to maintain health, are the important causes of the high price of food. Many times the present amount of food might be obtained, with no increase of the proportional cost, if the people would be content with a diet containing the different articles of food in that proportion which will allow the land to be employed in the production of those commodities for which it is best fitted; and the same food would supply many times the present population if it were only used to preserve health, and not consumed in administering to an appetite for intoxicating drinks or otherwise wasted through ignorance and a lack of appreciation of what inexclusive pleasures are.

In addition to these limitations of the food-supply caused by ignorance and prejudice, there are still greater contractions of the field of employment produced by the lack of appreciation of future as contrasted with present rewards, and hence capital is not accumulated to the proper amount, and the resources of all countries are but partially developed. To emigrate to new countries also requires capital, and where wages are low and the people ignorant, they have not the means, and often not even the desire, to go where wages are high and food is cheap. Thus the very fact that the price of food is high prevents the increase of food, as it causes an unfavorable distribution of wealth and an increase of ignorance, and prevents such a distribution of population as would increase the supply of food and remedy the unequal distribution of wealth.

In this connection only a reference can be made to another important cause of the high price of food, as a subsequent chapter will be devoted to its discussion. When there is free competition, the power of producers to survive does not depend on the gross produce of industry, nor on the efficiency of their labor, but on the surplus which can be given as rent. If the produce of one class of laborers is but one-half that of another class, the first class will displace the second if they demand less than one-half the wages. As the wants of cheap and inefficient laborers are small, and their rate of increase is rapid, they have the power of under-selling when furnished with capital at a low rate of interest. Paying a higher price for food, and more as rent, they drive the more efficient classes out of the field of employment, and at the same time they so re-duce both the gross return for industry and the field of employment itself that a much smaller population can be supplied with food than would be supported by the more efficient laborers whom they have displaced.

For these reasons it is evident that food is high in price not because any limit to the food-supply has been reached, but because the field of employment is so small to the ignorant and inefficient classes demanding the wrong commodities, and not willing to save for themselves. The obstacles to the increase of food and population are not physical in their nature. They are the result of ignorance and prejudice, and so long as they continue to flourish in their present force there cannot but be a high price for food and an unequal distribution of wealth.

From the foregoing discussion it will be seen a high price of food is not the result of a pressure of popula-tion against the means of subsistence that could be utilized if men were willing to conform to the condi-tions imposed by nature for the increase of the food-supply. Men impose unnatural limitations on them-selves, and thus limit their field of employment, and as a result they must pay a high price for food. Men have a tendency to reduce their food-supply below their actual wants, and thus cause an artificial pressure of population upon the means of subsistence which they are willing to utilize.

This tendency to limit the food-supply is true not only of man, but of all animal life. The pressure of the increase of animal life is not on all the means of subsistence, but only on those kinds of food which can be obtained under simple conditions. To use two or more sources of food requires more intelligence and a higher organism than does the use of but one kind of food. An abundance of food induces animals to use only those kinds of food which can be obtained with the least effort, and these are the varieties of food which can be obtained under the simplest conditions. For food obtained under simple conditions a simple organism is the fittest organism, and the instincts which accompany a low form of organic life lead the animal to reject all sources of nourishment except those whose conditions are so simple that only a small effort will supply its wants. Animals, as well as man, have a tendency to economize labor, and an economy of effort causes a decline of intelligence where the wants of an animal can be supplied under simple conditions. The simpler the organism the higher is its rate of increase, and the increase in numbers soon causes a pressure upon the means of subsistence which are utilized. The tendency to increase and the tendency to limit the food-supply are thus brought into conflict, and as a result in those animals in which these tendencies are weakest, some of the instincts and habits which limit the food-supply are broken down and a new species is formed, with a more complex organism, capable of acquiring more kinds of food, or the same food under more varied conditions. The simplest organisms, not the fittest organisms, tend to survive. Only when the increase of simple organisms have exhausted the food-supply that can be obtained under simple conditions will animal life develop and maintain the more complex organisms and that intelligence necessary for their existence where food can be obtained only under complex conditions.

Evolution does not arise from a primary tendency in animal life for the fittest to survive. It is the result of two apparently injurious tendencies,—the tendency to increase and the tendency to limit the food-supply. These two tendencies, always operating together, cause the simpler organisms in whom these tendencies are strongest to monopolize the means of subsistence obtainable under simple conditions, thus forcing those animals in whom these tendencies are weaker into more complex environments, where higher organisms and more intelligence are needed.

In the original man the tendency to limit the food-supply can be clearly seen, and in all the various social states through which he has developed up to the present time he has never failed so to limit the supply of food as to check the natural growth of population, and thus bring about an unequal distribution of wealth. The uncivilized races have numberless superstitions about food by which a large part of it must be rejected, and thus the supply is reduced. Each tribe will not eat cattle of a certain color. Here striped cattle are prohibited by one superstition; there the spotted animals are for a similar reason rejected, and travellers among such tribes often have great difficulty in feeding their followers, as no one kind of food can be procured which all will eat. Large quantities of food are given by these tribes to their idols or gods; and often their departed ancestors, being supposed still to relish food, must be conciliated by having a portion of what there is to eat set aside for them. At the same time the production of food is greatly limited by other usages and customs, which prevent the use of many tracts of land which otherwise would probably be cultivated.

When these tribes develop into nations having a higher civilization they lose many of these superstitions and customs limiting the food-supply, but others are retained, or adopted, which prevent the use of the greater part of the resources offered by the land of the country for the production of food. There is a strong tendency merely to utilize some one, or at least but very few, of the resources which might be developed. Some nations subsist only on the cattle which they herd, others cultivate some one plant, like rice or potatoes, which grow almost spontaneously in some regions, and still others live almost entirely on bread and meat, neglecting, and often despising, the many other means of subsistence which nature has placed at their disposal.

The original man was a slave to his appetites and passions, and enjoyed only those pleasures which are of a physical nature. As he did not conform in the least to the demands of nature, he had only those means of subsistence, such as berries, fish, and game, which nature furnishes without labor. A partial conformity to nature has caused the cultivation of naturally fertile land where the obstacles to cultivation are few. Here, however, the progress of civilization has been stopped, because no race has yet been willing to subordinate the physical and exclusive pleasures of life to those obtained from the consumption of other kinds of wealth which would so harmonize with all the demands of nature as to allow the use of all land in the most productive manner, and thus cause the removal of the more formidable obstacles to the extension of cultivation.

There is an obvious connection between the field of employment open to any people and the number of qualities in them which are sufficiently developed to influence their consumption. To those who desire but few things which thrive without labor the land of any country can furnish only a small supply of food, and to get this food they must live in small tribes separated so widely from one another that little commerce or division of labor is possible. As the development of the qualities inherent in men cause an appreciation of new modes of consumption, the land is gradually put to more productive uses. Additional men can be employed in agriculture, and the better cultivation of the land will allow a greater proportion of the whole population to be engaged in other work than the production of food. The development of each additional quality in men causes them to value new qualities in land capable of increasing their sources of enjoyment, induces them to economize food so as to be better able to satisfy their new desires, and leads them to a better appreciation of the future, which makes them willing to accumulate more capital and acquire additional skill. It may be truly said that the development of each additional quality puts mankind in a new world. With its aid not only is a new field of employment discovered, but the old one has a different aspect, since all its qualities are valued from an altered and more rational stand-point. Just as the use of larger and more powerful telescopes continually brings into view many-fold more stars than were before visible, and at the same time gives a new and more perfect view of those formerly observed, so also the gradual bringing into activity of new qualities in men causes a great increase of the opportunities to labor, and an enlarged return for labor in the field of employment before in use.

The greater the conformity to nature the more will all the qualities in land be brought into use, and the larger will be the ratio of the good land to the poor. On the other hand, when any nation endeavors to increase production without a greater conformity to natural conditions on the part of the people, there will be an increasing proportion of poor land as compared with the good. A nation first cultivates those soils which are considered by the people to be the best, and these are always those where food can be obtained under the most simple conditions. If their estimate of the land does not change on account of a better adjustment of themselves to nature, they can supply the wants of an increasing population only from soils less fitted than those before in use for the production of the commodities desired by those not conforming to nature. Only the development of those qualities in man which change his estimate of land, will cause an increase both of the quantity of land cultivated and of the ratio of the good land to the poor, allowing all land to be used for what it is best fitted.

From the qualities of the soil alone cannot be determined whether or not a given tract of land is good land. The demand for food and the use which is made of capital and skill are likewise important factors in determining our estimate of land. For this reason rent, when accompanied by a high price of food, is not the result of a natural monopoly. It is caused by the survival of classes or races who, contrary to nature, endeavor to use the whole world for the production of a few articles of food of which but small quantities can be grown, and who adhere to methods of production which economize to the greatest extent possible the use of capital and skill. When such men survive, a greater conformity to natural conditions being thus prevented, land less productive of the desired articles of food must be cultivated as the demand for food increases. The present high price of food and the artificial pressure of population on the means of subsistence are due to this lack of conformity to nature, and only by a better adjustment to natural conditions can we hope to preserve a low price of food and increase the average return for labor.

CHAPTER III.

THE LAW OF POPULATION.

An intelligent discussion of the doctrine of Malthus, which affirms that population tends naturally to increase faster than the means of subsistence, requires an accurate understanding of the terms and the method of proof used in this famous law. The whole controversy depends on the meaning of the terms natural and means of subsistence, and on the method employed to establish what is natural and what are the correct indications of the exhaustion of the food-supply. I have already discussed the limits of the increase of the food-supply, and have shown that there are two very different limits, the ultimate and highest productivity of the whole world and the practical limit determined by the amount of knowledge and capital possessed by mankind. What the whole world can produce and what may be obtained from the field of employment which the knowledge and capital of mankind allows them to occupy, are clearly independent problems, and require very different treatment. In his argument, Malthus overlooks the point of greatest importance, namely, the influence which the means used to increase subsist-

ence has on the increase of population. An increase
of food obtained without the aid of man would doubtless have no effect on his rate of increase, yet when the
co-operation of man is required to increase subsistence,
the changes brought about by the new environments
required to procure additional food might alter the
whole nature of man. That population tends to increase faster than the means of subsistence prepared *for*
it, does not prove a tendency to increase faster than the
means of subsistence prepared *by* it. There is a small
amount of produce prepared for man, and a large
amount that can be prepared by him with the aid of
knowledge and capital. Beyond a doubt population
tends to increase rapidly where the field of employment
is small, little or no skill and capital being required,
but this fact does not decide that such an increase is
natural to a society in the very different environments
necessary to make the whole earth its field of employment.

First, then, how are we to know whether this cause
is natural or not? The method of proof used by
Malthus is well known; to discover the natural
strength of the tendency of population to increase, he
considers its effect when comparatively unimpeded by
principles of an opposite tendency. He found that in
new colonies, where the tendency has the fewest checks,
population frequently doubled itself in twenty-five

years, and then concluded that this rate of increase represented the natural force of the tendency, and that this was the rate at which population always tends to increase. There are many objections to this method of reasoning which will quickly appear when we apply it to the investigation of other subjects. Suppose that we wished to determine the natural tendency of men to steal. If the Malthusian method is correct, we ought to find a place where the theft tendency is unrestrained by opposing principles. Unfortunately, we should not have to search long to find places where people steal as naturally and constantly as new colonies increase in population. And what conclusion can we legitimately draw from this? According to Malthus, we must conclude that all men are natural thieves, and that thieving would be as common as eating but for the fear of consequences.

By the same method of reasoning we could prove that all men are natural drunkards, cannibals, adulterers, and murderers, since we find communities in various parts of the world where drunkenness, cannibalism, etc., are common. The method is necessarily faulty, as it overlooks the fact that time and circumstances ultimately will change our desires and characters so completely that we learn to love a line of conduct which formerly would have been most unpleasant to us, and disliking what we formerly desired, what is natural of one time and place becomes most unnatural of another.

In every part of economic investigation the term natural is used not to denote what men would do if unrestrained by any surrounding circumstances, but to denote what they will do in given external circumstances if they are allowed a free choice. Under some circumstances they will naturally do one thing, and under other circumstances other things. It is not because it is natural that Americans buy cloth of England. It is natural to do that by which the greatest return may be obtained for their labor, and when they can obtain their cloth with the smallest expenditure of labor by exchanging with England they are inclined to do it.

The mistake of Malthus is the same as that of Ricardo in the natural rate of wages. There is always a rate of wages which will be just sufficient to support the laborer and bring up a new generation to supply their places, and this, says Ricardo, is the natural rate of wages. More wages would cause a too rapid increase of population, and a fall of wages to the natural rate; while a smaller rate would decrease the number of laborers and thus cause a rise of wages. Why were economists compelled to abandon this view? Because it overlooked the fact that what is natural changes with the intelligence and moral character of the laborers and with changes in political and social institutions. Economists rightly say, we cannot affirm what the laborers will naturally do unless we know all about the surrounding circumstances.

The distinction between the lessening of the tendency to overpopulate and the checking of this tendency can be well illustrated by the grades on a railroad. So long as the grades exist all hinderances to free movement of the train are checks to the tendency of the train to move, but any change in the level of the track by which the grade is reduced will lessen the tendency of the train to move down-grade, and the track being brought to a level, the train will have no tendency to move. There are in the present social state many causes influencing men to increase population, and whatever counteracts these causes is a check to its increase. Any change in the social state which will remove these causes lessens the tendency to overpopulate, and if they should all be removed there would be no such tendency, and hence no need of checks.

Malthus overlooks completely those causes which lessen the tendency to increase or incorrectly classes these with moral restraint. Our tastes and inclinations change with alterations in our ideas or surroundings, and what is natural in one group of circumstances is most unnatural in another. As an example take the tendency to drink spirituous liquor, which is at present almost as powerful and universal as the tendency to increase population. Where liquor is in common use and desired by all, if any one, believing it hurtful, should resist his inclinations and cease to drink, the effort could be properly classed as a moral check to the tendency to drink. If, however, his children were so educated as to have an aversion to its use, having no desire for stimulants, moral restraint is not needed to keep them from drinking. Children, having no tendency to use liquor, need no restraint, while the father, having a tendency, needs a moral restraint. The changes in the desires and appetites in the case of drinking illustrate what is gradually being brought about in regard to overpopulation. With the progress of civilization circumstances arise which reduce the inclination to marry, and even the power to propagate the race, and these altered surroundings cannot be classed either among moral restraints nor among any other kind of checks to overpopulating, since by them the need of any checks is removed.

It is now often asserted that the doctrine of Malthus has at length been settled beyond controversy by the discoveries of Darwin, showing the tendency of mankind to increase beyond the means of subsistence to be only a particular instance of a general law pervading all organic beings. There being in all organic life a

7*

capacity to increase in a geometrical ratio, any species of animal could in a small number of years overspread every region of the earth which had a climate suitable for its existence. Certainly there is a seeming unison in these two doctrines, yet a closer examination will reveal a lack of harmony. The view of man which Malthus takes is of that nature in which all species of animals were in his time regarded. Man was thought to have a definite set of attributes, which were unalterable and unmodified by change in surrounding circumstances. The doctrine of Darwin is the very opposite of this, the surrounding circumstances determining all the characteristics of animals, the latter changing with the former. If reasoning on the Malthusian plan, Darwin would proceed as follows: What is the natural rate of increase inherent in all animals? For its discovery the race of animals must be taken which has the most rapid rate of increase, this being the race where the natural rate of increase is least impeded by principles of an opposing character. The natural rate of this species being determined, it is then concluded that all other animals would have this rate but for the above-mentioned opposing principles. Such a method is necessarily absurd, there being no natural rate of increase inherent in all animals. Every species having its own rate, if we are to consider them as all having a common parentage, then we must also decide that the rate of increase of each animal, along with other peculiarities, is the result of its environments, and that it changes as these are altered or modified. If man is no exception to the general law of animal life, his rate of increase must also be determined by his surroundings and change with them, and there being no natural rate for all mankind, each society must be studied in its peculiar environments if we would discover the rate of increase.

Each animal is adapted to certain climatic conditions and kinds of food. The climate being favorable and the food abundant, the tendency to increase is strong, and the animal spreads over all the territory suited to it and provided with a supply of the desired food. Having reached its limit its spread and increase are stopped, but that does not show that all the means of subsistence are exhausted. Where is there an animal whose range is as extensive as of the things on which it subsists? Are lions and tigers found everywhere that deer or other similar animals exist? Certainly not. Clearly, then, the lack of subsistence cannot be the cause why they do not spread and increase. The cause must be sought in the inability of the lion or tiger to adapt themselves to the more varied conditions of climate and the like. If these animals had more intelligence they doubtless could conform to the circumstances of more extended regions, where their prey is abundant, and in the want of intelligence rather than of subsistence can be seen the real limit of their increase.

In this connection there is yet a problem to investigate with reference to the meaning of the tendency of population to increase. There is a broad distinction between the tendency of mankind to propagate and a tendency of population to increase. The individuals of a society may have a strong tendency to propagate, and yet the society have no tendency to increase. There is a difference between the seed of a plant and a child. The ripe seed requires no help or sustenance from the plant, but provides for itself, while the child does need aid and food, and without them would perish. The simple tendency to propagate in plants, unaided and unopposed, would result in an increase of plants, but a similar tendency in mankind would not increase population. For a child to arrive at manhood parents must feel some love for children, and be willing to provide them with food and other necessities. However true it may be that all races have too strong a tendency to propagate, it is not true that all races have an equal tendency to cherish and provide for their off-spring. So weak are these tendencies usually, that the most stringent laws are necessary to compel parents to support and properly care for their children. There are besides these other causes which alter the tendency to increase population. Mankind is subject to many diseases that cannot be prevented. From climatic and other unavoidable causes many die prematurely, and by so much is the tendency to increase lessened. For these reasons, to know the tendency of population to increase in any place we must know much more than what is the natural tendency to propagate. We must also ascertain the love of parents for children, their willingness to provide for them, and the unavoidable dangers from disease and other circumstances. When we have found out these facts we can know the strength of the tendency to increase population, and if we further discover the rate at which the means of subsistence is enlarging, we can determine whether or not there is a tendency to overpopulate. The effect of a tendency to overpopulate is to augment through war, famine, and the increase of disease the premature deaths to such an extent as to cut off the surplus population. An examination of the various races of men will make it evident that the tendency to increase population at the present time, in most races at least, is so strong as to be detrimental, but this gives us no reason to infer, as does Malthus, that it is natural and constant, and that moral restraint will always be necessary to keep it from injuring society.

There is, however, a much greater objection to the method of investigation used by Malthus than the misuse of the word natural. He examined only what

f

kept population down, and disregarded the causes which led to an increase of production. No decision can be reached on the relation of population and the means of subsistence without an investigation both of the checks to population and of the causes of the increase of food. When this is done, it will be immediately perceived that Malthus has enumerated among his checks to population the causes why the food-supply increases at all. He affirms that prudence is a check to population. It is, however, to the exercise of prudence that all the increase of food is due. No civilization at all is possible without the use of capital, and how is it possible to obtain capital without the use of prudence? Why do men save and accumulate capital if not to better their condition? Yet Malthus classes this desire to better one's condition among checks to population. It is, however, the cause of all increase of the food-supply, since to it is due all capital and all increase of skill and knowledge. The so-called prudential checks are really not checks at all in the sense that they are a restraint on population. They allow and cause an increase of population, but at the same time they regulate it and make it slower than it tends to be where they are not in force. On the other hand, the tendency to increase, unrestrained by prudence, does not increase population, but decreases it. Prudence is required to obtain capital and skill, and where these are not population decreases instead of increases, on account of the limited field of employment possessed by societies who do not save or educate.

Malthus and all his followers assume, without any investigation, that the high price of food is caused by natural and not social obstacles to the increase of food, and that wherever there is a high price of food the supply is so nearly exhausted that an unjust distribution of wealth does not even aggregate the evils of overpopulation, but only causes them to be somewhat earlier felt than otherwise. There are many reasons for doubting this assumption, and I shall endeavor to show that there is no connection between a high price of food and the exhaustion of the food-supply, that a high price of food only occurs in those societies where the natural resources are undeveloped or wasted, and that it is only by so conforming to natural conditions as to allow a low price of food that a society can exist with intelligence and capital sufficient to exhaust the food-supply.

The only kind of a society where there is a pressure of population on the food-supply is in the original state where no capital is used, and where man only consumes what he finds, doing nothing to increase his means of subsistence. The amount of fruit, berries, eggs, and wild game is strictly limited, and population must limit itself to their amount, and if more persons are born than can be fed, they must die of starvation or disease. So long as the Indians live on buffaloes there is a ratio between their number and that of the buffaloes. With a given number of buffaloes only a given number of Indians can live, and whatever the food of people in such a state of society may be, the law is the same; as they do nothing to increase the food, they must limit themselves to their food by prudence, or suffer from want and disease and other positive checks to population. This, however, is all changed when men discover that they can increase the food-supply by labor exerted previous to the time of consumption. The labor expended before the produce is needed, we call capital; and so long as the return of labor can be increased by the use of capital the relation is that of population to capital, and not that of population to subsistence, as it was before. These very different relations are regarded by most economists as identical, and economists pass over from the conclusions derived from one of these relations to those of the other as if they were the same. Only so long as men merely consume and do not produce, can prudence act as a check to population, or be rightly regarded as a check. When men begin to produce by means of capital, prudence is no longer a check to population. It is the cause of its increase, since all capital is the result of the exercise of prudence, deferring consumption in order to enjoy increased consumption at some future time. In such a society there is on one hand the desire of immediate consumption, and on the other the desire for the increased consumption which can be obtained by deferred consumption, and on the comparative value of the present and the future depends the amount of population which can be supported. Whatever increases the regard for future welfare allows an increase of population, and whatever augments the desire for immediate consumption checks the increase of population.

Here, then, we have a very different view from that presented by Malthus. His prudential checks no longer operate as they did on the original society merely to check population. They now are the cause of its increase in opposition to the positive checks which render the future uncertain, and hence increase the desire for immediate consumption, and thus check the growth of population. As the desire for future consumption and the amount of capital increases, more land is cultivated, and a larger population can be supported, while the increase of population is checked by any increase of the desire of immediate consumption. Such a society is divided into two classes,—capitalists, who prefer an increased but deferred consumption, and the laborers, who choose immediate consumption. When labor tends to increase faster than capital the

8

rate of wages falls, and continues to fall, until the too rapid rate of increase of population is checked by the diminishing returns obtained for labor. In the rate of wages we have a criterion by which to determine the force of the tendency to overpopulate, for where wages are low the tendency is strong. The tendency to overpopulate, not overpopulation, is the cause of low wages. Where this tendency is strong and wages are low, labor being inefficient and unskilled, less is produced than if the tendency to overpopulate were weaker, and less being produced, and the produce less skilfully and more wastefully used, a smaller population can be supported than where the tendency to overpopulate being weaker, wages are high enough to enable the laborers to become intelligent and skilful.

I wish to emphasize the contradictions in which writers become involved when they confound two problems so essentially different. Mankind suffers from a want either of capital or food, one or the other, but not from want of both. The want of capital arises from social causes, the want of food from physical ones. In the latter case it is the niggardliness of nature which causes their suffering, in the former it is social and not natural causes which have prevented the increase of food and caused its high price. If the doctrine is correct that more capital will always employ additional labor, then it is not true that we are now pressing against the means of subsistence. By far the greater part of the world is yet open for the employment of capital, if it were obtainable. Besides, there never was a time in the world's history when the population was as well supplied with food and at so little outlay of labor as at the present time. By this, however, is not meant that the price of food is lower, for this is not true, but that a smaller proportion of the population is engaged in agriculture than ever before; and this, not the price of food, is the true test. On the other hand, the lack of capital is to be seen on every side. The rate of interest is not the proper criterion of the plentifulness of capital. A low rate of interest only means that capital can be obtained at a low rate by those who can give good security; the mass of mankind cannot give this security, their desire for immediate enjoyment being so strong that they will neither save for themselves nor prudently invest capital which others would willingly place in their hands if capitalists were sure that they would use it properly.

The societies in which the price of food is high are those in which the people are divided into separate classes, capitalists and laborers. The laborers not being under the necessity of exercising prudence, increase rapidly, while the rapid increase of capital lowers the rate of interest; and the result of these two influences is a rise in the price of food and a fall in the value of other commodities,—changes which transfer the greater part of the revenues of the country to the landlords. In such a country only cheap labor and capitalists willing to save at a low rate of interest can survive, for such a combination can force the price of food so high, and the price of other commodities so low, as to displace the other and better classes, who cannot offer to landlords such favorable terms. Here we have a high price of food, and at the same time an ignorant and inefficient population tending to increase too rapidly. This only shows that there are social causes which allow the ignorant part of the population to survive. Hence the seemingly universal proposition of Malthus is really but a particular one, no account being taken of the rate of increase of the classes which the social arrangement permits to be displaced by their inferiors. The high price of food in such a society comes from a limit to the field of employment open to surviving combinations of cheap labor and low interest. This furnishes no indication of an exhaustion of the food-supply. The prevailing prejudice and ignorance cause the available resources to be but partially used, and prevent whole countries from being inhabited at all.

The preceding arguments show that the high price of food is not the result of natural laws, but of ignorance, prejudice, and an unequal distribution of wealth. To this Prof. Cairnes objects thus:

" It matters not whether the obstacles be physical or natural, whether absolute and insuperable, or the result simply of prejudice and ignorance, so long as they are effectual in preventing the cultivation of the countries in question. So long as this is the case these countries, to all practical intents and purposes, may be said not to exist for us. They can no more be counted on as means of supporting a population than the countries in the moon."

What Prof. Cairnes shows is that uncultivated countries and other unused resources are of no practical account so long as the ignorance and prejudice remain, but that is not what he and other Malthusians set out to prove. Their original proposition is that population naturally tends to increase faster than subsistence, while what they make out is that population increases too rapidly where ignorance and prejudice cause an ill distribution of wealth. The best way to show the weakness of Prof. Cairnes's argument is to apply his reasoning another way. Besides food men need water, both to drink and for cleanliness, and just as valid a ratio can be shown between the increase of population and the supply of water as between population and the supply of food. Population increases according to a geometrical ratio, while the supply of water at best only increases in an arithmetical ratio, and the effect of bringing together the two different rates of increase

8*

will be just as striking as the contrasting of the increase of population and that of subsistence. So we must conclude that population naturally increases faster than the water-supply, and that the amount of population is always proportional to the supply of water. Certainly the lack of cleanliness has caused many times more deaths than the lack of food ever caused, and the fact that men die from lack of cleanliness shows that the supply of water has been exhausted. It is, however, objected that the brooks and rivers are full of water, which could have been used but for the ignorance of the people and their prejudice against cleanliness, and that many times the present population might be supplied with water if they would go to the brooks and rivers to get it. To this Prof. Cairnes, if consistent, would reply, that it matters not whether the obstacles are physical or moral, or the result simply of prejudice and ignorance, so long as they are effectual in preventing the bringing and using of the water; and that so long as this is the case these brooks and rivers, to all practical purposes, may be said not to exist for us.

The argument that the increase of population is checked from want of water is certainly as well-founded as the argument that population is checked from want of food, and any argument ever brought forward to prove one position can be equally well applied to prove the other. All that can rightly be inferred from either proposition is that so long as ignorance and prejudice have their present force, the whole supply of either food or water cannot be utilized, great suffering is produced, and population remains much less than it would otherwise be. Outside of this question of what people will do when swayed by ignorance and prejudice, there is a problem of great importance. What are the real limitations of the increase of food and water? To the solution of this problem neither Malthus nor any of his followers has made any important contribution. From all their arguments it could not be inferred whether the real limits of the increase of mankind will be a want of water or of food, for their conclusions merely show that there must be a limit to population, and not what that limit is.

The mistake of Malthus was that he investigated only the rate of possible increase inherent in those classes who do nothing to increase the food-supply, and neglected to examine the influence on the increase of population of those conditions by which the food-supply is increased. To these conditions men must conform if population is to increase, and the question of importance is what men naturally do who comply with the conditions necessary to increase the food-supply, and not what men will do who will not adapt themselves to the environments necessary to a high civilization. The latter class must pass away if civilization progresses, and their places be supplied by others who better conform to natural conditions. Only those can remain who appreciate the future enough to accumulate capital, and will use the food which nature supplies most abundantly, and who will consume food only as a means to preserve health, and take their pleasures in such a manner as is most conformable to the general good. It is only by such as these that the world can be fully populated; and so long as men do not show these characteristics the population of the world must remain small in proportion to what it might otherwise be, and the distribution of wealth will be so unfavorable as to cause a low rate of wages and a high price of food.

Only as the development of the qualities in men opens up to them new sources of pleasure will they adjust themselves better to nature and increase the food-supply. So long as the appetites and passions of men have their original force, those means of enjoyment which afford an immediate pleasure will be preferred to those that augment the pleasures of the future rather than those of the present. The original man takes his pleasure to-day, putting off his burdens and pains until to-morrow. On the other hand, he who conforms to nature takes up his burdens to-day and enjoys a much greater stock of pleasures on the morrow. He produces before he consumes, while his ancestor consumed before

he produced. The supply of food can be increased only
as men learn to place the pain before the pleasure, and
those qualities which must become active in men before
they will place production ahead of consumption will
also cause them to prefer pleasures having no painful
reaction to those like the pleasures tending to increase
of population, which have so many undesirable consequences. The conditions allowing the increase of
food can be complied with only as production is placed
further and further ahead of consumption. This will
be done only as the qualities leading men to prefer deferred to immediate pleasures gradually become more
developed, and as they develop the original appetites
and passions become weaker.

We can thus determine beforehand in what manner
the very nature of man must be altered to utilize all
of the productive forces of nature. Those habits and
customs which limit the food-supply must be broken
down, those appetites and passions which cause men to
prefer immediate to deferred pleasures must be weak-
ened or lost, and the desire of exclusive pleasures must
be displaced by a love of those pleasures whose enjoyment does not exclude the mutual enjoyment of others.
Just as the course of a river is fixed by the slope of the
land through which it flows, so the natural conditions
which surround man determine what changes in his
pleasures must be made and what qualities in him must

be developed before an increased quantity of food can be obtained for a growing population. The tendency to overpopulate must be reduced to comply with the conditions for enlarging the means of subsistence, and there is no reason to believe that the rate of increase of those who conform to the natural conditions by which they are surrounded will be greater than their means to increase the food-supply.

CHAPTER IV.

THE produce of a country is divided into three parts, rent, profits, and wages; these being the terms used to denote the reward received by the landlords, capitalists, and laborers for the assistance rendered by each to production. If this be correct, to know what the share of any one factor is, it would seem necessary to know what the shares of both the other factors are. To know what the amount of wages is, it must be known what is the amount of both rent and profits, or to determine what profits are, we must know the amount of rent and wages. The current theory of wages and profits does not recognize this relation, but proceeds to determine wages and profits without any reference to rent. Wages, we are told, depend upon profits, rising as profits fall, and falling as profits rise. John Stuart Mill, in his discussion of profits, puts the case as follows:

"It thus appears that the two elements on which, and which alone, the gains of capitalists depend, are,

95

first, the magnitude of the produce; in other words, the productive power of labor; and, secondly, the proportion of that produce obtained by the laborers themselves; the ratio which the remuneration of the laborers bears to the amount they produce. These two things form the data for determining the gross amount divided as profit among all the capitalists of the country; but the rate of profit, the percentage on the capital, depends only on the second of the two elements, the laborer's proportional share, and not on the amount to be shared. If the produce of labor were doubled, and the laborers· obtained the same proportional share as before,—that is, if their remuneration was also doubled,—the capitalists, it is true, would gain twice as much; but as they would have had to advance twice as much, the rate of their profit would be only the same as before."

If whatever of the ultimate produce of industry is not profit is wages, from what source do the landlords receive their share? Certainly from some source they obtain a large revenue, and where could they get it if all the produce of labor goes to increase wages and profits? The importance of this question is not overlooked by Mill, but he claims that no practical error is produced by disregarding rent, and promises to show this in a subsequent chapter on rent to which he refers. To this explanation I wish to call especial attention, because the correctness of Mill's position is of the greatest importance both in the discussion of wages and also of free-trade.

As is well known, these subjects were elucidated by Adam Smith before the law of rent was known. All his demonstrations rest on the supposition that produce is divided into two shares only, wages and profits, whatever is not resolvable into one of these elements being resolvable into the other. When the law of rent was discovered by Ricardo, it being evident, that produce was divided into three shares instead of two, the greater part of Political Economy was worked over and rent put in its proper place. This, however, was not done in the discussion of wages or of free-trade. These subjects still continue to be discussed as though there were only two factors among whom the produce of industry is to be divided, and rent is either ignored or eliminated from the discussion. The latter is the method employed by Mill, and if the reasoning by which he accomplishes this is unsubstantial, all his discussion of wages, as well as free-trade, is defective. The element of rent must be introduced and the course of reasoning modified to meet the altered conditions before correct results can be obtained.

I quote in full Mill's explanation, given at the close of his chapter on rent, of the reason that no practical error arises in disregarding rent and supposing that all the advances of the capitalists consist in the wages of the laborers.

"After this view of the nature and causes of rent, let us turn back to the subject of profits, and bring up for reconsideration one of the propositions laid down in the last chapter. We there stated that the advances of the capitalist, or in other words, the expenses of production, consist solely in wages of labor, that whatever portion of the outlay is not wages is previous profit, and whatever is not previous profit is wages. Rent, however, being an element which it is impossible to resolve into either wages or profit, we were obliged for the moment to assume that the capitalist is not required to pay rent,—to give an equivalent for the use of an appropriated natural agent,—and I undertook to show in the proper place that this is an allowable supposition, and that rent does not really form any part of the expenses of production, or of the advances of the capitalist. The grounds on which this assertion were made are now apparent. It is true that all tenant farmers and many other classes of producers pay rent. But we have now seen that whoever cultivates land paying a rent for it, gets in return for his rent an instrument of superior power to other instruments of the same kind for which no rent is paid. The superiority of the instrument is in exact proportion to the rent paid for it. If a few persons had steam-engines of

superior power to all others in existence, but limited
by physical laws to a number short of the demand, the
rent which a manufacturer would be willing to pay for
one of these steam-engines could not be looked upon
as an addition to his outlay, because by the use of it
he would save in his other expenses the equivalent of
what it cost him; without it he could not do the same
quantity of work unless at an additional expense equal
to the rent. The same thing is true of land. The
real expenses of production are those incurred on the
worst land, or by the capital employed in the least
favorable circumstances. This land or capital pays, as
we have seen, no rent, but the expenses to which it is
subject cause all other land or agricultural capital to be
subjected to an equivalent expense in the form of rent.
Whoever does pay rent gets back its full value in
extra advantages, and the rent which he pays does not
place him in a worse position than, but only in the
same position as, his fellow-producer who pays no rent,
but whose instrument is one of inferior efficiency."

Notice the difference between what Mill starts out to
prove and what he finally succeeds in showing: "The
advances of the capitalist consist solely in wages of
labor, and whatever portion of the outlay is not wages
is previous profit." This is what he was to show, but
the proposition which he does prove is very different
from this: "Whoever does pay rent gets back its full

value in extra advantages, and the rent which he has to pay does not place him in a worse position than, but only in the same position as, his fellow-producer who pays no rent."

What Mill succeeds in proving is merely that it makes no difference to the capitalist whether he pays rent or wages. Whether wages go down and rent goes up, or wages rise and rent falls, is all the same to the capitalist. His profits and advances are not affected by a change which causes the shares of one factor to be diminished if at the same time the other proportionally increases.

A few examples will illustrate clearly the insufficiency of Mill's argument. Let us suppose two sections of a country having an equal amount of agricultural produce, and in one of them the land is of unequal fertility, the rent being equal to one-quarter of the produce, while in the other all the land has the same fertility of the poorest land in the first section, and hence no rent is paid. In this case the advances of the capitalists in the first section would be three-quarters to the laborers and one-quarter to the landlords, while in the second all the advances would go to the laborers. The amount advanced in each case would be the same, as the amount of the produce is the same. The recipients, however, are different, and for each seventy-five laborers employed in the first section one hundred laborers would be employed in the second. Mill is right in saying that it is all the same to the capitalist whether he hires seventy-five laborers and pays an amount equal to the wages of twenty-five laborers to landlords or employs one hundred laborers and pays no rent. Yet this does not show that all the advances of the capitalist in the first case consist in wages of the laborers. The landlord coming in the place of twenty-five laborers gets their wages, and the result to the capitalist is just the same as if these laborers had been employed and no rent paid. The landlord is a nominal laborer, who, doing no work, receives his share of the produce along with the real laborers who do the work. Of course it is the amount of the advances, and not who gets them, that interests the capitalist; but Mill promised to prove an entirely different proposition, namely, that all the advances of the capitalists went to the laborers. This proposition, which is necessary to maintain his position on the wages question, he did not prove; he merely stated it and then passed to the discussion of another point.

The error involved in disregarding rent becomes evident when we consider the nature of the doctrine established by disregarding it. Mill wishes to establish the fact that wages fall as profits rise, and rise as profits fall. By these terms are meant not the absolute, but the proportional share received by each. The rate of profit, we are told, depends upon the laborer's proportional share, and not on the amount to be shared. A proportional share of the produce certainly goes to rent even if no rent is paid on some part of the produce. If thirty per cent. of one-fourth of the produce is rent, twenty per cent. of the second fourth, ten per cent. of the third, and none of the fourth, then fifteen per cent. of the whole produce is rent, just as much as if fifteen per cent. of every part of the produce is rent. The advances of the capitalists would be the same in one instance as in the other, and hence it is evident that the rate of profit cannot be determined by knowing the proportional share of the laborer alone, but only when the proportional shares of both laborers and landlords are known.

There is still another method of showing that Mill's position is incorrect. He asserts that if the produce of industry were doubled and the laborers obtained the same proportional share as before, the rate of profit would also remain the same, not being increased at all. Let us suppose that, the land of two grades being cultivated, each grade producing a half of the food-supply, there was difference enough in their productivity to give ten per cent. of the whole produce of industry to the owners of the better land as rent, and that of the remaining produce the laborers received seventy per cent., leaving twenty per cent. as profit. If the produce of industry were doubled the better grade of land would now produce enough to supply the whole demand for food, and rents would fall to zero. The laborers receiving the same proportional share as before (seventy per cent.), profits would be raised from twenty to thirty per cent. I have taken this simple case to make the falsity of Mill's argument more evident, yet the same result would follow in more complex cases. To be sure, if the produce of land were doubled all rent would not disappear, still no one can doubt that such an increase of produce would reduce rent. Even if it were not reduced in amount, its proportional share would be less, since if ten per cent. were rent before the doubling of the produce, the landlords receiving none of the additional produce, rent would now be but five per cent. of the whole return for labor, and, the laborers receiving seventy per cent. as before, profits would be raised to twenty-five per cent., a gain of five per cent.

In his chapter on ultimate analysis of the cost of production, Mill again endeavors to prove the dependence of wages on profits by showing that the value of any commodity is determined not by wages, but solely by the quantity of labor which it costs to produce that commodity and bring it to market.

"The value of one thing," he says, "must always be understood relatively to some other thing, or to things in general. Now, the relation of one thing to another cannot be altered by any cause which affects them both alike. A rise or fall of general wages is a fact which affects all commodities in the same manner, and therefore affords no reason why they should exchange for each other in one rather than in another proportion. To suppose that high wages make high values is to suppose that there can be no such thing as general high values. But this is a contradiction in terms, the high value of some things is synonymous with the low value of others."

The fallacy in this argument arises from the use of the term commodity with two meanings. With one meaning it denotes everything bought or sold, while with the other its use is restricted to those articles capable of indefinite increase, whose values are determined by the quantity of labor necessary to produce them. If all commodities could be made in any quantity desired without an increase of cost, a rise of wages affecting all commodities alike could not influence values. There are, however, many commodities, of which the articles of food are the most important, whose values are not determined by the quantity of labor necessary to produce them. If one-third of the labor of a country is devoted to agriculture and two-thirds to other commodities, one-half of these commodities will not usually have as great a value as the agricultural produce, yet they are the produce of an equal amount of labor. Indeed, it might easily happen that the value of the agricultural produce might exceed the whole value of all the other labor.

There being two classes of commodities, the value of one depending, the value of the other not depending, on the quantity of labor required to produce them, the value of one class can increase at the expense of the other. Such a change not affecting all commodities in a like manner, a rise in the rate of wages would increase the value of those commodities whose cost depends on the quantity of labor necessary to produce them, and decrease the value of the other class of commodities, composed of food and the like. It is easy to illustrate how these changes are brought about. There being no rent in a new colony, when the best land only is cultivated, all commodities, including food, will exchange in proportion to the labor needed to produce them. When, however, the increased demand for food requires the cultivation of inferior land, the agricultural produce will not exchange with other commodities in the same ratio as before. A bushel of wheat will exchange for more cloth, cutlery, or other like articles than when no rent was paid. As rent is raised through the resort to inferior lands to supply the increasing demand for food, a bushel of wheat will gradually exchange for more and more cloth, and the greater the value of the wheat the less will be the value of the cloth and other commodities whose values depend solely on the quantity of labor needed for their production. On the value of these latter commodities depends the rate of wages, and it will fall as the value of agricultural produce rises and rent absorbs a greater part of the whole produce of industry. Supposing one hundred yards of cloth to be the result of one week's labor, and the same work to be necessary to produce ten bushels of wheat on the best land, so long as no rent is paid they will have an equal value, and a week's wages will be equal in value to ten bushels of wheat. When inferior land is brought into cultivation, producing but nine bushels of wheat for the same labor that will give a return of ten bushels on the best land, one hundred yards of cloth will exchange for nine bushels, and the wages of all workmen per week will be nine bushels, this being the amount for which the produce of a week's labor (one hundred yards of cloth) will exchange. The cultivation of still poorer lands being required, on which the labor of one week will produce but eight or seven or a still less number of bushels, wages will decline to a like amount.

The produce of industry and the rate of interest remaining unaltered, a rise of wages would reduce the value of food, and raise in a like degree the value of other commodities. A rise of wages would, to use a term of Mill and his school, throw out of cultivation the poorer lands and raise the margin of cultivation, and in this way the value of food would fall and that of other commodities would rise. The effect, then, of a fall of both wages and interest, or a fall of either one, the other remaining unchanged, is to increase the value of food and other raw material, and to decrease the value of other commodities; in other words, to cause an approximation of the value of food and other raw material to the value of those commodities produced by their consumption. If five bushels of wheat and ten pounds of cotton are consumed in the production of one hundred yards of cloth, wages and interest will depend on the value of wheat and cotton. While twenty yards of cloth will exchange for the above amount of wheat and cotton, eighty yards will remain to be distributed as wages and interest, but as the value of wheat and cotton increases so that first thirty, then forty or more, of the hundred yards of cloth must be given in exchange for them, the return for labor and capital is reduced by a like amount. It is, then, the margin between the value of what is consumed in production and what is produced, on which wages and interest depend, and they increase as the margin is enlarged. In other words, the return for labor and capital depends on the approximation of the value of food and raw material to that of finished commodities. As both wages and interest fall, or as one of them falls, the other being unaffected, the margin will be less and the approximation be greater, while the margin will be increased and the approximation decreased by a rise of either wages or interest, or of both of them. This is the effect of a change of wages on values, and a rise of wages not affecting all commodities in a like manner, all those propositions which affirm that the rate of profit depends on wages are incorrect, and Mill's attempts to save the propositions of the older economists, who elucidated the theory of distribution as if there were but two factors,—wages and profits,—are failures. He only succeeds in giving a false coloring to many economic truths, which, while confusing his own views and those of the reader, renders the true laws and relations of distribution clouded and invisible.

If we are to obtain a correct statement of the laws of wages, it can only be done by placing rent in its proper place as one of the factors of distribution, investigating not only the relations of wages and profits, but also of wages and rent. In other words, it must be determined what are the conditions according to which wages can rise at the expense of either profits or rent, or when to their benefit wages will fall.

So long as the number of laborers is so small that all can be employed on lands of the best quality, the rate of wages depends upon profits, but when population increases, so that the supply of food is no longer obtained at the lowest cost, from any limitation to the field of employment, rent arises. Now there being three factors in the distribution of produce, the possibility of raising wages no longer is limited to the questionable possibility of reducing profits; for wages under these circumstances can rise as well by a reduction of rent as of profits.

I have in the previous chapters discussed the nature of rent and the effect that a change of the demand for commodities has on rent, and the fallacies of the current view on this subject. I now wish to show the effect which a change in the demand for commodities has on the possibility of a rise of wages at the expense of rent. If, as the price of food becomes higher, poor lands are converted into good lands, and there is not, as is commonly asserted, an inexhaustible supply of poorer and poorer lands that can be brought into cultivation as the price of food increases, then, as the community progresses, the proportion of good lands to the poor lands increases, and the greater part of the produce is obtained from good lands.

Let us suppose two nations having an equal supply of food, in one of which one-half the food is produced on land that yields no rent, while on the other only one-tenth of the produce is furnished by such lands. It is plain that in these cases there would be a great difference in the power of the laborers to reduce rent by economizing food. It would doubtless be impossible in the first case for the laborers to accomplish anything. So great a reduction as one-half in the consumption of food would doubtless be beyond their powers. If, however, only one-tenth of the food was produced on lands yielding no rent, this reduction could be easily accomplished, and their wages increased by the fall of rent.

The ratio of good lands to the poor is, then, the all-important factor in determining the possibility of an increase of wages. If all the lands are good and yield rent, as they do in most old countries, then there is the possibility of a much higher rate of wages, if the laborers will consent to the proper method to obtain the increase. That as the price of food declines the supply decreases but little, is manifest from the results of American competition on English agriculture. No land has been thrown out of cultivation in England by the fall of prices, nor has the quantity of food produced been reduced. The same fact was plainly shown by the small effect of the late hard times in reducing the food-supply, while the fact that the laborers did not suffer seriously for want of food shows that they can, if they really desire, reduce their consumption of food to such a degree as to produce a low price of food. As low a price can at any time again be obtained by a

reduction of their consumption, either through a better economy of what they eat or a reduction in the
amount wasted in drink; all alcoholic drinks being
made from food-stuffs, and requiring much more land
to be cultivated than would otherwise be necessary.
If it requires a million acres to produce the food consumed in the manufacture of liquor, then if its consumption ceased either a million acres of poor land
could be thrown out of cultivation, if there be poor
lands in cultivation, or if not, these acres could be used
to produce food. On either supposition there would be
a marked reduction in the price of food. The same
objection holds to the use of tobacco as to the use of
liquor. The land used for this purpose either contracts
the area used for the production of food, or requires the
cultivation of a much poorer class of lands. In either
case a rise of rent and a reduction of wages follow.

Laborers are continually trying, usually with ill
success, to increase their wages, but no endeavor is
made to reduce the price of those articles which they
wish to purchase with their wages, although here they
have a field where they could produce great effects if
they would use the same energy which they display in
their contests with capital. If they succeed in obtaining higher wages, it is questionable whether their real
wages are increased. They always endeavor to obtain
food and drink with their increased wages, and the

rise in price of these articles so much reduces the value of their wages that little or none of the increase is left. This is clearly shown by the rise in the price of food accompanying the rise of wages at the end of the crisis of 1873. Every advance of wages was accompanied by a like advance of rent in its various forms, so that now the laborers are little or no better off than before. No better plan for the benefit of landlords could be devised than to have wages increased, since the laborers always adopt a course of action that only ends in transferring their wages to the landlords.

It is remarkable that laborers do not stop their discussion of wages long enough to consider what must be the inevitable result, whatever their wages may be, so long as they expend their money in the present manner. How much more food does each family obtain now than before the late rise of wages, and how much less house-room does each family now have than they had when a few years ago rents were one-half their present rate? If these and other similar questions were asked and discussed, it would show how little the supply of food and houses is enlarged by the rise in the price of food and in the rent of houses. The increased price of these alters the distribution of wealth, but has little influence on its production in as far as it affects articles demanded by the laborers. The laborers are attempting to do an impossible thing, since while the mass of the wealth produced is the result of their labor, they all want only the produce of the labor of but a small portion of their number. ʹTwo-thirds of them are employed in other pursuits than agriculture, and still most laborers refuse to consume anything else than agricultural produce. While this is the case they will get the result of only one-third of their labor, no matter what their nominal wages be. Their determination to get food and drink for all their wages will cause the value of food to rise, so that all their wages will purchase only the necessary food and what they drink.

The laborers have also other resources besides this for raising wages at the expense of rent. They can change their consumption of food from articles which nature produces scantily to those produced more abundantly, or they can consume more of articles produced in climates of which the best lands are as yet not wholly occupied, and consume less freely of articles from places where the demand for their produce is so great as to cause much rent to be paid. This problem has already been discussed in the chapter on the social causes producing a high price for food, and hence a single example is needed to show its bearings on the rate of wages.

A demand for whiskey or beer is a demand for a class of lands already in use and on which high rent is paid, and this rent will be further increased by the demand for whiskey or beer, since these drinks are made from the common cereals used for food. On the other hand, a demand for coffee is a demand for another class of lands of which but a small portion is in use. A change of demand from whiskey and beer to coffee would much reduce the rent of lands on which the common cereals are grown, while much more coffee could be produced without a material increase in price. Hence the whole gain in the reduction of rent on the grain-producing lands would come to the laborers as increased wages. The use of liquor, and other means by which the food-supply is wasted, is not merely a destruction of capital, which only interests the consumers, their families and friends. If the demand for food when no liquor was drunk would cause the price of wheat to be one dollar per bushel, while the increased demand caused by the use of strong drink raise the price to one dollar and twenty-five cents, by compelling a resort to poorer lands, then all persons, even those who do not drink, lose twenty-five cents on every bushel they consume, since they are forced to pay that much more for their food than they would otherwise have to do.

In saying that the demand should be changed from articles like wheat to those like corn, potatoes, or rice, of which much more can be produced on the same ground, I do not mean to infer that the use of wheat

should cease. The demand for wheat is so great that
the supply cannot be obtained from the land for which
it is best adapted ; and when land better fitted for other
crops is sown to wheat, the price of wheat rises to such
a point that the cultivation of poorer land is profitable.
This, of course, causes all the better wheat lands to
pay higher rent, while if a less amount of wheat were
demanded, its price would fall and wages rise. Climatic conditions fix the number of good acres for wheat,
corn, rice, and all other articles, and when each acre
is devoted to what it is best fitted, the price of all kinds
of food is low and wages are high. Nature will not
change to suit our notions; we must conform to her
laws. So long as the food of a people is composed of
a few articles, like wheat and beef, wages must be low,
since a demand for them alone causes such a waste of
the productive forces of nature that but little is produced, and from that little much is taken as rent.

The tendencies of our present civilization having as
an effect the concentration of all industry in a few
places to which all others are tributary, the question
necessarily arises whether this concentration has any
effect upon the rate of wages. If we suppose, as is
often the case, that on account of the close proximity
of coal and iron some one point has a real advantage
over every other place in a country for producing iron,
and so much advantage that it is the interest of every

other place that their iron be produced at this point, what would be the effect on the distribution of wealth as place after place were induced to obtain their iron here in exchange for their products? A little consideration will make it plain that wages must fall. Those places that were nearest would have the greatest advantage in the exchange, and while trade was carried on with them only, wages would be high, as at every point there is a like efficiency of labor, and of rent there would be none. When, however, more distant points began to trade in the place, wages must fall enough to equal the cost of transportation. The whole labor used to produce the iron and carry it to these more distant points and bring back their products would be less efficient than that employed in making exchanges with the nearer points. There cannot be two rates of wages in the same market, and hence the wages of all must sink to the lower rate. If a ton of iron would exchange on the home market for thirty bushels of wheat, and it cost five bushels of wheat to transport it to a more distant point and bring back wheat in exchange, as soon as this trade begins the ton of iron must exchange for twenty-five bushels of wheat at the home market. As still more distant points made their exchanges at this place, the price of iron must still further decline, and that of wheat go up, which is the same as a reduction of wages. If wages did not go down the exchange could not be made, and wages must continue to decline as long as more and more distant points continue to be brought into commercial relations.

The decline of wages is the condition on which such a trade can be carried on, no matter what be the aggregate gain to the nation at large. To illustrate more generally, let us suppose a city to be formed in a fertile plain, from which population extended out on all sides, the conditions of trade being such that it were advantageous to manufacture and trade in this one place, what was lost in cost of transportation being made up by more efficient production by manufacturing on a large scale. As production extended farther and farther from the city the cost of transportation would be greater at each extension of cultivation, and the price of food would rise and that of other commodities fall, and by so much would wages be reduced. While according to our supposition the gross produce is in proportion to the number of laborers employed, and as great as ever, still wages must decline, since some portions of that labor are less efficient than others, and with free competition no laborer can obtain more than those least productively occupied.

The gains of any of the laborers from the advantages of production on a large scale and of foreign trade cannot be greater than those of the laborers who are least benefited, and this is the same as saying that they obtain no benefit, the most disadvantageously located having but nominal gains in the exchange.

If the commerce and industry settles in two or more cities, the difference in the efficiency of labor is less, and wages will be higher than if all industry were congregated at one city. The larger the number of the cities and the better the distribution of the population, the greater will be the rate of wages, the difference in the efficiency of labor being less; and the smaller this difference (the gross product of labor being the same) the greater will be the wages and the less will be the rent. The landlords as a class are interested in having the population congregated in as few places as possible; the welfare of the laborers, on the other hand, is furthered by anything which causes a better distribution of population and brings them nearer the producers of food.

If the laborers ever advance far enough to investigate the causes which determine the prices of the articles which they consume, they will see how much more powerful a lever for increasing real wages they have in combining to influence the price of food than in combining to increase money wages. The increase of money wages is at best but small, for it reduces the profit of capital. To economize the food-supply, to cause a better distribution of population, and to change the demand of food so as to reduce rent, not only raise wages but also profits, and enable capital so to increase as to employ more labor, not only increasing, therefore, the wages of labor but also the demand for labor.

Production is limited by the field of employment, and every change by which food is saved and used, not for pleasure but only to preserve health, or by which the products of the whole world are more fully demanded, increases the field of employment and enables more capital and labor to be employed and raises both wages and profits.

There is one other point of importance in determining wages to which it is necessary to refer, namely, the condition of the agricultural population. So long as they are in a miserable condition, and through defective laws are deprived of the protection needed for the prosecution of their industry, the amount of produce will be small compared with what it should be. Thus the field of employment and production is limited, and wages fall both through the limit to production and through the influx to the cities of country labor seeking employment. It is not probable that the laborers of the cities if left to themselves would increase in numbers faster than the food-supply should, but when the country population is ignorant or deprived of their natural rights, the result cannot but be disastrous to the laborers of the cities, who not only must compete with the surplus country population, but must also, from the ignorance prevailing in the country, have their food-supply lessened. Laborers who wish high wages must be careful to do all in their power to place the lands of the country in the hands of those who will produce the most, to aid the spread of education among the country population, and to change the laws of the nation so that those who improve lands shall have proper protection. Only by these and like means can the increase of the food-supply be made rapid enough to supply the demands of an increasing population without an increase of rent. Every true reform must begin with measures relieving the agricultural classes of their burdens. A rise of wages cannot precede, but must follow the decline in the price of food. It is only when the laws sufficiently encourage the growth of intelligence among the agricultural classes that they can displace all the obstacles to the increase of food, and make all land that should be cultivated of so high a degree of fertility that the price of food would fall below the cost of production on the best lands now in use. Then rent will become a very subordinate element in the distribution of wealth, and labor and abstinence will have their proper reward.

CHAPTER V.

FREE COMPETITION.

THE advantages of free exchange and competition are obvious, and have been often explained and exemplified by economists of all schools, but the disadvantages have been entirely overlooked, or deemed so subordinate as not to be worthy of attention. Most economists boldly declare that a state of freedom, both in domestic and foreign exchange, is always beneficial to all parties, and that interference on the part of the state does incalculable injury. As to the benefit of free foreign trade, there is, of course, a wide difference of opinion, but the benefits of free competition in domestic trade are almost universally regarded as beyond dispute. Yet the subject of free competition really involves all those issues which are so earnestly discussed under the head of foreign exchange, and a solution of the difficulties of the latter problem cannot be obtained till the benefits and injuries of free competition in domestic exchange have been determined. If it be asked why free competition is beneficial, the ready answer is, it causes everything to be produced where it can be made at the lowest rate, and wherever commodities are cheapest, the least labor has been employed in their production. Both protectionists and free-traders use the criterion of cheapness to determine the advantages of exchange. If a protectionist be asked why his system is superior, he will doubtless reply that it makes everything cheaper, and he will quote statistics to show how much iron, cotton, cloth, and other commodities have fallen in price since the introduction of a high tariff.

This criterion of cheapness is clearly and tersely set forth by John Stuart Mill, while treating of the relative merits of production on a large and small scale.

" Wherever there are large and small establishments in the same business, that one of the two which in existing circumstances carries on the production at greatest advantage will be able to undersell the other. The power of permanently underselling can only, generally speaking, be derived from increased effectiveness of labor; and this, when obtained by a more extended division of employment, or by a classification tending to a better economy of skill, always implies a greater produce from the same labor, and not merely the same ·produce from less labor; it increases not the surplus only, but the gross produce of industry."

In this passage we have the issue plainly presented. Cheapness, the power of permanently underselling, is

an unfailing test of the advantages of different systems
of production. If an article is produced and sold
cheaper by one system than by another, it indicates a
more efficient use of labor, a better economy of skill,
and, lastly, which is most important of all, a greater
produce from the same labor. If increased efficiency
of labor is the only cause of a reduction of prices, wages
and profits can have no effect on the value of commodities. Wages must go up as profits go down, and profits
rise as wages fall; each exactly counterbalancing the
effect of the other, they produce no change in prices.
Is this correct? Are there no commodities that change
in price when profits fluctuate? If a lowering of
profits were always attended by an increase of the real
reward of the laborers, Mill's view would be correct,
but when the two fall conjointly because the price of
food has risen through a limit to the field of production being reached, commodities do not exchange at the
same values as before. A mere statement of the case
shows that the price of food could not rise unless food
exchanged for all other commodities in a new proportion. It does not follow that there has been no change
in the value of commodities because there has been no
change in profits. The real reward of the laborers may
fall and the price of food rise without affecting profits,
but any change in the relation of the two by which
the rate of profits is not altered must have an effect

on prices, and in so far as this should happen prices would be affected by something else than the efficiency of labor, and the power to undersell would depend not on this efficiency alone, as is claimed by Mill, but also on the wages of labor and the price of food.

Prices are affected by those changes in wages caused by the competition of one class of laborers with another. Some classes of laborers have greater efficiency than others; but if they require more wages than the others, it is a problem for the capitalist to determine which is more advantageous for him to employ. If the first class have double the efficiency, and demand less than double the wages, they are cheaper to him than the second class; but if the first class demand more than double the wages, the second class will be more profitable to the capitalist. So long as there is work for both classes all can get employment, but as population increases and the limit of the field of industry is reached, all cannot get work, and then the question arises, which class will survive? Unquestionably it will be the class of laborers that cost their employers the least, for those capitalists who pay the least in proportion to the efficiency of their laborers can undersell their competitors.

In every country there are many classes of laborers, who vary much in efficiency and in the amount of wages requisite for their needs and support. In his discussion of normal values, Prof. Cairnes, having clearly shown the existence of these various classes, seeks to determine the ratio at which the commodities of one class exchange with those of other classes. While the importance of this discussion is conceded, there is a much more important question to which I wish to call attention, namely, what determines the relative numbers of the various classes. Prof. Cairnes calls them non-competing groups, but this is true only from one point of view. There is some reason why the lower classes of laborers cannot do the work of the higher, for if no obstacle stood in the way they would compete, and the wages of all classes be the same. The higher and more skilful classes, however, can do the work of the lower classes, can do it much more skilfully than the lower classes, and get a much greater return from the same labor. A mechanic, for instance, could plough, sow, and do other farm-work much better than the ordinary farm-hand. He has greater intelligence, and, with a little practice, would have greater efficiency in farm-work. So, too, those classes, having more skill and intelligence than the mechanic, can perform his work much better than he; but he cannot compete with them in their work. The reason, then, why the higher classes cannot drive out the lower classes from all occupations is not because they cannot do the work of the lower classes.

They can do it, and much more efficiently than it is now done. It is because they would demand so much higher wages that the cost of labor would be greater than it now is.

It is here in the competition of different classes of laborers that wages have an effect on prices. Any work that the lower classes can do is done by them, not because they are more efficient, but because they demand less wages in proportion to their efficiency than the higher classes. The capitalist employing the lower class of laborers under these conditions can sell cheaper than his rivals, and if one capitalist makes use of a low class of labor the others must do likewise, or be driven out of the market. As a country grows older and the field of employment becomes more fully occupied, the higher classes of laborers are driven from one employment after another, until, at last, they perform only such labor as the lower classes cannot do. When there is a surplus of laborers, the desire to undersell causes the substitution as much as possible of the lower classes for the higher and more skilful. In some cases the substitution is complete and all of the higher classes are driven out. Usually they do not all lose employment, only their relative numbers being diminished, and thus the cost of production is reduced.

This suggests the reason why the introduction of

machinery and production on a large scale is so profitable. They require for their operation a much smaller number of the higher classes in proportion to the whole number of the laborers employed. When machinery is introduced the work of the laborer is much more simple than before, and requires less skill. Likewise when the scale of an industry is enlarged, there being a greater division of labor, much less skill and versatility are required of each laborer. In both cases a lower class of laborers can be employed, and the products can be sold cheaper. The gross produce of industry, however, is much less than it would be if none of the lower classes were employed, since a given quantity of food will not support a greater number of the lower classes than of the higher, while the efficiency of the higher classes, being much greater, will cause much more to be produced.

The manufacture of pins is generally used to illustrate the so-called advantage of a better economy of skill arising from the substitution of unskilled labor for the skilled. It is said that the wages now paid in England for making pins vary from four pence to four shillings a day, and if four shillings a day were paid to skilled laborers for doing all the work, the price of pins would be more than three times as high as it now is and there would be a serious waste, as labor is most efficient in production when each individual is employed upon work best suited to his skill and physical strength. This argument would be good if there were no limit to the food-supply, if all laborers could be employed, and if there were no competition among laborers for places. Whenever the field of employment is fully occupied, every laborer of a higher class who is driven out of one occupation by the employment of laborers of a lower class is excluded entirely from employment, or at least the relative number of his class employed is reduced, and the gross product of industry is diminished according as his efficiency surpasses that of the laborer displacing him. Inventions and discoveries are constantly being made by which the average return for labor is increased, and every such improvement renders possible the employment of a greater proportion of dear but efficient labor. Yet the tendency is just the opposite. Less use is made of skilled labor when the employment of machinery and production on a large scale allow a greater division of labor, a continually smaller proportion of skilled labor being employed as the use of machinery becomes more extended and the scale of production is enlarged. The effect of a substitution of cheap for skilled labor must be detrimental when the average return of the industry in which skilled labor is economized is less than the average return for all labor. It is not proven that the wages of skilled labor in the manufacture of pins (four shillings a day) is greater than the average return for all English labor, and hence it cannot rightly be inferred that the more extended use of skilled labor in this case would be a serious waste, or that the gross produce of English industry would thereby be reduced.

The power of underselling is not, as is claimed by Mill, due always to the greater efficiency of labor; on the contrary, the power is usually obtained by the substitution of cheap labor for that which is more efficient but dearer. The cheapness caused by the employment of low-priced labor is not universal; a low price of the products of labor is produced, but a high one for food, the increase in the price of food going to the landlords as rent. When the price of food is so low that every laborer receives the whole produce of his labor, the laborers of the higher classes receive enough to supply themselves not only with food, but with other useful and necessary things. As soon as the competition of laborers caused by a surplus of labor begins, the question arises not who can produce the most, but who can spare the most to buy food with. The class which can do this survives, and the others either disappear, or only remain in places where circumstances prevent competition from affecting their wages.

The lower classes can almost always, if they are not prevented by some circumstances in the nature of the

i

industry, or by some legal restraint, displace the higher, just as poor money drives out the good. There is no more reason to believe that capitalists will employ efficient labor, if its cost is high, than to believe that they will meet their own obligations with costly money when poor but cheap money would do as well. Cheap money will drive out the good, and cheap labor, the efficient, except in cases where cheap labor and cheap money are excluded by circumstances or law.

If we further take into consideration the causes determining who shall cultivate the land, the case of cheap labor becomes still worse. As the question of survival in other occupations rests not on the ability to produce the most, but on the ability to pay the highest price for food, so in agriculture the question is not who can produce the greatest quantity of food, but who can pay the most rent. The public welfare demands that the greatest possible quantity of food be produced, but the landlords are interested only in rent, which is the net produce, and they, not the public, decide who shall cultivate the lands. If we suppose two competing classes of laborers, one having ten per cent. less efficiency of labor and requiring eleven per cent. less wages than the other, this less efficient labor will displace the dearer. The gross industry of the country will be reduced ten per cent. provided the same number of laborers as formerly could be supplied with food.

But the same number cannot be supported, for the cheap labor now being used in agriculture will be ten per cent. less efficient than the dearer labor formerly employed, and will therefore produce ten per cent. less food. Hence but ninety per cent. of the former population can be supported, and as each individual is ten per cent. less efficient, the production will be but eighty-one per cent. of the amount formerly produced, making a deduction of nineteen per cent. in the gross produce of the country in order to give the landlords one per cent. more than they formerly received.

There is yet another cause for the displacement of skilled labor on a large scale in the change in the demand for commodities which the survival of a low class of laborers occasions. Cheap and poorly-made commodities can be made on a large scale of production more advantageously than can the dearer and better-made articles ; custom-made boots, ready-made clothing, cheap jewelry, and other like commodities which a low class of laborers desire, are the result of production on a large scale. On the other hand, the finer articles of apparel, costly ornaments, works of art, and most of the other commodities sought after by persons of means and refinement, are hand-made, and require a high class of laborers for their production. A low class of laborers will demand the produce of a low class of labor, and whenever they displace a high class of laborers from one occupation by accepting a lower rate of wages, they displace others of the high class of laborers by a change in their demand for commodities which require the cheap instead of the dearer and better made articles to be produced.

At the same time a low class of laborers, through their exclusive demand for a few articles of food, reduce the food-supply. The amount of food that can be produced depends on what is desired, and when there is a demand for only a few articles of food, but a mere fraction can be produced of what could otherwise be obtained if the variety best suited to natural conditions were demanded. When, also, there is only a demand for a few articles of food, a much lower class of laborers can be employed in agriculture than would be the case if a greater variety were desired. It requires much greater skill on the part of the farmers to cultivate a great variety of crops than it does to raise a single crop, and where the work is simple, a low and ignorant class of laborers can survive. Thus one displacement of skilled workmen causes another, and wherever the cheap laborers once begin to drive out the skilled they soon get possession of most occupations, both through the change in the demand for commodities and through the increase in production on a large scale.

In comparing two methods of production to determine which of the two will have the greater gross production economists usually regard only the productive powers of the workmen, and overlook the effect of different modes of consumption on the gross amount that will be produced. If A can produce more yards of cloth in a day than B, the inference is immediately drawn that if A displaces B the gross produce of the country will be increased. Yet this conclusion is likely to be erroneous, and certainly the reasoning is defective. The main element in determining the gross produce of any country is the use which is made of the land and the economy of the food-supply. Nature can produce some articles of food more abundantly than others, and some men take their pleasures in a way that will cause a greater consumption of food than do the habits of other men. A difference of fifty per cent. in productive power would be an uncommon superiority of one class of laborers over another, while of many articles of food the land of a country produces a many-fold greater quantity than of other kinds of food, and the difference in the economy of food consumed by different persons is even greater than the difference in their productive power.

Let us suppose that A produces fifty per cent. more of any manufactured commodity than B, and that B consumes those kinds of food of which the same land and labor can produce twice as much. Then twice the number of persons like B can be supported by a country, and with the same average income which persons like A would have, provided that in a nation of people like A half the people were engaged in agriculture. In a nation of A's one man produces enough food for two men, while in a nation of B's one man can produce sufficient food for four persons, the land being twice as productive of the articles which men like B desire. As a result, three of the four men can be spared from agriculture for other work. A being fifty per cent. more productive in manufacturing than B, can, we will suppose, produce six yards of some commodity in a day, while B can produce only four yards. A must give half of every six yards in exchange for food, one-half the laborers in his society being agriculturists, and has three yards remaining for his own use. B, however, gives but one-fourth of his four yards for food, only that portion of the workmen of his nation being agriculturists, and hence has also three yards remaining. The average income of each person in both societies will therefore be the same,—food and the equivalent of three yards of cloth for each day's work. Yet when men like A survive, the gross produce will be but one-half of what it would have been if men like B had displaced those like A.

This proves that the gross produce of any nation is mainly determined by the economy and the consumption of food, and not by the greater productivity in manufacturing. At the same time the average income of a people consuming the articles of food more easily produced, will be as great, if not greater, than that of the other nation, a much smaller proportion of the laborers being engaged in agriculture. The fact that those who consume the articles of food less easily produced is admitted only as an illustration, since it accords with the commonly-accepted doctrine that the cheapest producer is most productive. I contend, however, that the opposite is true, those workmen being most productive in all industries who conform to the natural conditions by which they are surrounded. They will have developed in them a greater number of the qualities given to them by nature, and they are most efficient who have the greatest number of active qualities developed, and not they who sell their produce at the cheapest rate.

The evil results arising from a low rate of interest are possibly more detrimental to the increase of industry than those produced by a fall of wages. When the rate of interest has fallen so low that the greater portion of the people no longer have sufficient inducement to save, society being divided into two classes, capitalists and laborers, the rate of interest is then mainly determined by two considerations,—the accumulation of wealth and the capitalist's place of residence. The richer the individual the easier it is for him to save.

This point has been so often observed and illustrated that it only needs to be stated, but the other consideration, the place of residence of the capitalist, will require considerable illustration, as its effect on the rate of interest has been entirely overlooked by most economists.

The rate of interest is not the only consideration which influences the capitalist to save; he is also largely influenced by the purchasing power of money. If money will purchase more at one time than at another, the rate of interest will be lower during the first period than during the second, for the same money will better supply the wants of the capitalist; or, in other words, the same wants can be supplied with less money. Hence, when the increase of capital reduces interest, capitalists will save for a lower rate of interest than they would if the value of money was not so great. Just so the place of residence of the capitalist influences the rate of interest, money having different values in different places. A capitalist in a place where he can buy what he wants cheap has an advantage over those who, from their location, must pay more for what they desire. When the pressure from an increase of capital comes, those most advantageously situated will submit to the greatest fall in the rate of interest, the same interest having more value to them than to others in unfavorable situations, who will, as a class, either cease to save or remove to more advantageous situations.

For a capitalist a city offers more advantages than the country. In the country, it is true, food is cheaper than in the city, but this constitutes but a small share of the capitalist's expenditure, and in all other respects the city offers the better inducements.

Another important consideration to the capitalist is the rate of wages. If wages are low, those articles of which his consumption mainly consists will be lower than where wages are high, as the greater part of what he consumes is manufactured commodities. These articles fall in price as wages fall, and places where wages are low extend advantages to capitalists which other places where wages are high cannot offer. As a country grows in wealth and the rate of interest falls, the advantages of the best place of residence will have additional weight with the capitalists. The country will be more and more drained of its capital by the gradual but constant movement of its capitalists to cities which offer better advantages to capitalists for enjoying their incomes, and from these sections of the country and cities where the rate of wages is high to those where the wages are low.

It is almost needless to mention that the same influences which induce capitalists to congregate in cities and in places where wages are low, operate with equal force on the landlords of a country. While the capitalists and landlords derive their revenues from different economic sources, still, as wealth accumulates and interest falls, both the capital and land of a country fall into the hands of the same class of persons; that is, those who will save for the least consideration. These in the long run will be those who, from the advantages of situation and from the concentration of wealth in the hands of a few persons, can force the rate of interest to so low a point that to all others the inducement to save becomes insufficient.

When it is asserted that the landlords will remove to large cities, those holding the legal title are not always meant, but often those who are the virtual owners, the holders of mortgages. Whenever land is mortgaged the real landlord is not the farmer who owns the land, for his share is usually not more, and is often much less, than the amount of capital employed on the place in buildings and improvements. The real landlord is he who holds the mortgage, and he need not reside near the land, but may live wherever his desire or fancy dictates.

The influence of these considerations on the capitalist class, and consequent gradual concentration of wealth in a few places and in the hands of fewer and fewer persons, may be observed everywhere, and nowhere plainer than in the United States. Every year sees the country lose more and more of its capital, and the land fall into the hands of persons who, even if they retain the nominal ownership, are not its real owners. They are merely laborers, who have little or no hope of ever becoming the real owners, since the price of land is so high that the interest eats up all the profits of the farmer. One by one those farmers who are out of debt dispose of their farms and remove to the neighboring towns and cities, and their places are supplied by those who have no time for amusement and care little for churches or schools. Thus whole sections are gradually becoming stripped of their wealth, and are inhabited only by families whose necessities compel unceasing labor for scant returns, and deprive them of the leisure necessary to the making of intelligent, thinking citizens, while those who really enjoy the produce of the land live often hundreds of miles away, and have no interest or concern in the prosperity of the places whence come their revenues.

The causes which really underlie the misery of Ireland, the absenteeism of its landlords, are at work in our own country, and will in time produce the same sad results; we then shall have on our hands not merely one Ireland, but a country full of Irelands, the tillers and occupants of the land sending away all they produce and receiving little or nothing in return.

While capitalists are located everywhere throughout the country, there is good ground to believe that any local advantage for the investment of capital will be utilized. Industries will then be carried on mainly in the places where food is cheapest. Labor will naturally gravitate thither, food being the laborer's chief article of consumption. All this is changed by the localization of capital and its concentration in the hands of a few persons knowing or caring little for the advantages which other places than those now utilized may possess for carrying on trade or for manufacturing. So long, for instance, as Wales or Ireland has local capitalists eager to invest their money, there is good ground for assurance that the advantages of these countries will be developed, but after they are once drained of capitalists and landlords, the remnant lacking energy, and only with great difficulty meeting their obligations, the fact that certain industries are carried on at Sheffield and Manchester is not evidence that these cities have natural advantages not possessed by Ireland or Wales.

After the land of a country is all in use, the only way to increase the produce of industry is by improving the land and educating the laborers. Capital when held by a few persons wanting only safe investments, never adopts either of these modes of extending production. If land to any extent is to be improved, it must be done by those who live and labor upon it, and from their own earnings; and if the laborers are to get any education they must pay for it themselves, unless, perchance, the government provides it. For these reasons laborers on land are usually ignorant and inefficient, the land is but partially improved, and production is checked by an artificial limitation to the field of employment, brought about by the rate of interest sinking so low that only a few persons most advantageously situated have sufficient inducement to save.

In such a social state the laborers will be congregated in large numbers in the few places most attractive to the capitalists. Wherever the capitalists go the laborers must follow. Most of the food will be sent to the capitalists owning land for rent, and the workmen must leave their old homes and seek the food. Just as a swarm of bees must follow the queen bee, moving when she moves, and stopping when she stops, so must the mass of the people not saving for themselves follow after the few who possess capital, and congregate in swarms where the capitalists reside.

Those who have not all the qualities necessary for production are dependent on those who have all that is required, and the greater the dependence of any class the less will their interests influence production. If we had a telescope large enough to discover the size and number of the cities in distant planets, we could determine the prevailing rate of interest. The larger the cities, and the fewer their number, the greater the accumulation of wealth and the lower is the rate of interest. Whenever a nation favors a low rate of interest and the accumulation of wealth in the hands of a few persons, a great deterioration of the laboring classes is sure to follow. On one hand, they lose the inducement to save, and the qualities which a high rate of interest tend to develop. On the other hand, by being crowded together in large cities, they lose many means of enjoyment which were free to them when scattered throughout the country. Pure air, the beauties of nature, and the many innocent rural sports are lost, and all the remaining pleasures are those exclusive ones derived from the consumption of liquor, tobacco, and other rude enjoyments attractive only to persons deprived of other pleasures.

As has been shown in a former chapter, the value of agricultural and mineral products is liable to sudden changes, since a slight increase in the demand for these articles must cause so great a rise in their price before the supply can be increased from new land and mines with great obstacles to their use, while a slight decrease in the demand will cause a very low price, there being no land or mines in use having a great cost of production, which will go out of use as soon as the price of these products begins to fall. The suddenness and extent of fluctuation in value of all commodities are greatly increased as soon as production on a large scale, combined with a low rate of interest, causes the laborers

who would save to be displaced by those having no
desire to save for themselves. When the price of any
article falls those who have capital lay up a stock of
the commodity, and thus the fall in value is checked
by the increase in the demand. Those who do not
save must reduce their purchases when prices fall.
The decline of prices reduces the amount of work to
be performed, and when no work can be obtained their
consumption of commodities must be reduced to a
minimum. When the mass of the laborers have no
capital, the decline in price of the produce of a few
industries causes a decline in the demand for all commodities through the reduced consumption of those
without work. All industries are affected, and through
the accumulated effect of the reduced demand for labor
in the various trades there is a sudden and a great
decline in the value of all commodities. On the other
hand, as soon as altered industrial circumstances offer
work to the laborers there is a sudden and rapid rise
of values, caused by the urgent needs of those laborers
who for a time have been compelled to do without many
of the necessaries of life. Production on a large scale,
and free-trade likewise, tends to increase the fluctuation
in values, since they cause the industries of the whole
world to be carried on in a few places, which are so intimately connected with one another that whatever affects one centre of trade reacts upon all other commer-

cial centres. So long as each nation was commercially independent, a decline in values in one country caused an increased export of commodities to other lands where prices were unchanged. When, however, all nations are intimately joined in commercial relations, no relief from a fall of values can be obtained by exportation of goods, since all parts of the commercial world being affected by similar circumstances suffer at the same time from a decline of values.

These causes of the fluctuation of values also affect the value of gold and silver, destroying that permanency of value which renders them so superior to other kinds of money as a medium of exchange. All writers who have advocated correct doctrines concerning money lay great stress on the fact that a decline in the value of the precious metals in one nation will cause them to be exported to other nations where their value is higher. This argument for the superiority of metallic money is of no importance where all nations are joined in such intimate commercial relation that they really form but one nation. Under these conditions the rise and decline of the value of the precious metals will happen at the same time all over the world. The same amount of money is not needed at all times, there being a greater amount of trade and commerce some years than others, yet the amount of money will be the same at all times, when the fact that all nations enjoy prosperity and suffer ill fortune together prevents such an exporting of the precious metals from one nation to another as would give them a greater stability of value.

In yet another way does the increase of cheap labor increase the fluctuation of the value of money. In former times, before independent workmen were displaced by production on a large scale, almost every workman possessed a hoard of money, which he enlarged when the value of money fell, and put into circulation when the value rose. A multitude of such hoards acted as a reservoir, preventing great changes in the value of money. By the displacement of producers on a small scale this reservoir has been lost. The laborer of to-day instead of possessing a hoard of money laid away for hard times, usually, by means of the credit system, spends his wages before they are earned. Wherever a low rate of interest induces business men as well as workmen to make an extensive use of their credit and economize the use of capital as much as possible by means of production on a large scale, all commodities, including money, will be subject to sudden changes in value. The extent of fluctuations of values has gradually increased as more extended use has been made of low interest and cheap labor, and when this combination has displaced all independent producers who save for themselves, these fluctuations of value will be so great as to render all production a lottery, and prevent every one from saving except those who have capital enough to control some industry.

The effect of low wages and low interest is an approximation of the price of raw material to that of manufactured commodities. As has been shown in the previous chapter, the reward of labor and abstinence is dependent upon the difference between the price of food and other raw materials and that of the finished commodities. The value of agricultural produce is low as compared with finished commodities when only those lands having great original fertility are tilled. As soon, however, as the supply of these lands is exhausted and others must be cultivated requiring the expenditure of capital to fit them for tillage, the approximation of prices begins. There is a class of capitalists who prefer safe investments and a low rate of interest, and a class of laborers who accept low wages rather than make the sacrifice necessary to become skilled and efficient or to save capital. To neither of these classes does the preparation of new lands for tillage offer any attraction, since such enterprises are not safe investments to capitalists, nor sought after by indolent, inefficient workmen. These two classes combining bid for the field of employment open to them, and there is only one method open for their success. In exchange for food and raw material they must offer a greater quantity of what they produce than can be done by the other class who are skilled and save for themselves. If ten yards of cloth is offered by the more efficient class for a bushel of wheat, this combination of low interest and cheap labor will give eleven, or a greater number of yards, and thus drive out their superiors by the approximation of the prices of raw material to manufactured articles which is in this manner brought about. There are no means by which any class of laborers or capitalists can escape the result of this approximation of prices. If one class of producers are willing to exchange twenty yards of calico for a bushel of wheat, all producers offering less for wheat lose their trade, while those offering twenty yards will be displaced as soon as a combination of cheaper labor and lower interest can give twenty-two yards for a bushel. In this way the approximation of prices becomes greater as a nation grows older, and as a result the intelligent classes are gradually displaced, and rent absorbs a large part of what is produced on the limited field of employment open to the surviving combination.

It is usually claimed that the competition of laborers benefits the capitalists, and that the competition of capitalists benefits laborers; but this we now see is not correct. So soon as a limit to the field of employment is reached the result of all competition, both of laborers and capitalists, is lower interest and lower wages, while rent is raised by the consequent approximation of the price of raw material to that of manufactured commodities.

It is objected, however, that laborers regain their loss from low wages in the lower prices at which they obtain what they consume of others' labor. So far as they are consumers of the commodities produced by other laborers, they lose and gain nothing, while all laborers lose by the increased value of food and raw material. Suppose three yards of silk, six yards of linen, or fifteen yards of calico could be exchanged for a bushel of wheat before the fall of interest and wages, and that afterwards four yards of silk, eight yards of linen, and twenty yards of calico were required to procure a bushel of wheat. If this were the case, the owners of wheat would make a gain of one-third in all their exchange for silk, linen, and calico, and the producers of these articles, while losing in all their exchanges for wheat, would be in the same position as formerly in regard to the exchange of the produce of one laborer for that of another laborer; that is, the ratio of exchange of silk for linen or calico, or calico for linen and silk, would be the same as before, a yard of silk still exchanging for two of linen and five of calico.

The increase of the value of wheat would not be the only gain of the landlords, for the same labor and capital as before would be willing to engage in production for one-third less return than formerly, so that agricultural capital and labor would be compelled to drop one-third of their remuneration. Thus the landlords would not only get one-third more for their wheat, but the wheat would be produced for them at one-third less cost than formerly.

Since the power of underselling does not necessarily arise from an increased efficiency of labor, and since between rival producers the question of surviving is determined not by the amount of gross produce, but by the amount of the surplus above interest and wages which can be given for rent, it is evident that production on a large scale is not adopted as the most economic method, but because it effects the largest utilization of cheap labor and low interest. It is essential to the success of production on a small scale, and of co-operation as well, that interest be high enough to induce every one to save, and that all the laborers be skilful and intelligent. But they cannot develop skill and intelligence if the reward for their labor is squeezed down to its lowest possible limits by the employment of cheap labor and low interest in production on a large scale. Let us suppose that three dollars a day is just sufficient to induce laborers to become skilled and save capital enough to furnish them with self-employment, and that by production on a large scale one-fourth less was produced, and at one-third less cost. In this case, although for every three hundred dollars' worth of goods formerly produced, only two hundred and twenty-five dollars' worth is now produced; yet as wages and interest have fallen one-third, what was formerly sold for three hundred dollars can now be obtained for two hundred and seventy-five dollars, or one-twelfth less than formerly. Skilled laborers must now work and save for two dollars and seventy-five cents a day, and since this is not enough to induce laborers to become skilled and save for themselves, they will be displaced by the producers on a large scale, and the gross produce of the country will be one-fourth less than before the displacement took place.

Of course the term production on a large scale must be used in a relative sense. What at one time would be regarded as a very large scale of production would at another time seem extremely small. The main point to be kept in view is, the advantages of cheap labor and low interest are so great that the scale of production is greatly extended in those cases where it is really beneficial, and in many cases where small combinations of laborers are most efficient, they are displaced by the use of cheap labor and low interest solely on account of the power of underselling which this combination possesses. For this reason the scale of production now employed is not a fit criterion for determining what method of production is most advantageous. Nor will a comparison of present methods with those formerly in use be any more decisive. The restoration of any former class of laborers is not what is desired, but the preservation and enlargement of that class thinking and saving for themselves who are now reduced to so small a number by the false economy of skill and intelligence.

CHAPTER VI.

ALL writers, in discussing the law of diminishing productiveness of the soil, have accepted, without dispute, the assumption that the return for labor from a given tract of land could be continually increased by the use of more labor, the point controverted having been whether or not the additional labor obtained a greater or a less proportional return than the previous labor. Both parties seem to have overlooked the third alternative, that the proportional return might increase up to a point beyond which no additional return could be obtained by any amount of labor. If this were true, we would have a law of limited returns as contrasted with a law of diminishing returns. Then, instead of a law asserting that a greater number of people cannot be as well provided for as a smaller, we should have the following: up to a given figure the greater number of people can be better provided for than the smaller, but a number of people exceeding that figure cannot be provided for at all. Against such a position the arguments used by the advocates of the law of diminishing returns would not be valid.

152

They argue that if the law of diminishing returns were not true, only the best soils would be cultivated. Poor soils are cultivated, and this would not be the case if the law of diminishing returns were not operative.

The cultivation of poorer soils and the high price of food are accounted for by the law of limited as well as by that of diminishing returns. If in the case of wheat the returns increased proportionally until sixty bushels to the acre were harvested, and none beyond this could be obtained by any amount of labor, additional acres would have to be cultivated as the demand for wheat increased; and when all the good land had been brought into use, inferior lands would have to be resorted to, and the price of wheat would rise owing to the increased cost of cultivation.

The fact that inferior lands are cultivated shows that the superior lands cannot supply the market, and that there is a limit to the productivity of land, but what that limit is this fact alone does not decide. If, up to this limit, land gives increased returns to the labor employed, and will yield nothing further without increased knowledge or improvements, then new and inferior lands would be cultivated as the demand for food increased just the same as if the law of diminishing returns were true. The only difference would be that some of the additional supply would be obtained from the old lands by the use of additional labor, if the law of diminishing returns were true; while, on the other supposition, all the increased supply would come from the new lands, unless the increased price would cause additional capital to be used or induce the farmers to use more skill and better methods.

So far at least as man subsists on animals the law is of limited and not of diminishing returns. The American Indians who lived on buffaloes did not suffer from a limited increase of their numbers, since they could hunt more successfully in large than in small numbers. When many hunted, so long as they only killed the increase of the buffaloes, they obtained a greater proportional return for their labor than when only a few engaged in the chase. When, however, they killed more than the increase of the buffaloes, their game became scarce, and they had to hunt longer than before and get less game. To Indians, then, as to all races who subsist on wild game, the law must be that of limited returns, an increase of population being beneficial so long as they do not reduce the number of animals on which they subsist; and they cannot increase their numbers at all beyond the number which consumes the increase of the animals constituting their food. The same law applies to fisheries; if more than the increase of fish be consumed, the labor of catching them is increased while the number caught is diminished. Still more is the law of limited returns true of people who live by herding domestic animals, such as cattle and sheep, since their labor decreases as the number of cattle or sheep increases, and as long as there is pasturage, an increase of population is beneficial; but when grass gives out the population cannot increase at all. So far then as population is supported by animal life alone the law of diminishing returns does not hold. If the law applies to anything it must be to the increase of vegetable life. When man resorts to agriculture for food, or to increase the food of the animals on which he subsists, the laws of the increase of food seem to be different from those by which it was governed when he lived on animal food alone. A correct analysis, however, of the causes by which vegetable life is increased will reveal the same law as that of limited returns.

If an ultimate limit to the increase of vegetable life on a given area can be shown, the truth of the law of limited returns will be made clear, provided it can also be shown that this limit can be reached without a decreasing proportional return to the labor employed. Such a limit to the increase of the food-supply may be found in the space needed by each plant for its proper growth and development. On any field only a certain number of plants of any kind can thrive, and if more are allowed to grow, the return will be diminished instead. of increased. If a farmer should sow eight bushels of oats or wheat to the acre, his return would not be so great as if he sowed only three or four bushels, the plants needing room, air, and sun to mature properly. The limit varies with different plants. If we sow a field to wheat and then to rye, we may increase the return by the change of plants, but every plant has its limit, and hence there must be a limit to the supply of vegetable food.

Inasmuch as the extreme limit to which production can be forced is that of space or room for the plants, the question whether the law of the return is that of limited or diminishing returns must depend upon what are the elements which contribute to the increase of vegetable life. If labor is the only or the chief element, then the law of diminishing returns might be true. If labor is subordinate to other elements of a very different nature, then we must expect to find that the law is that of limited returns.

The relation of the law of limited returns to knowledge and capital may be clearly stated in the following way. There is a greatest possible return from a given area; this return is seldom obtained, for it requires a conjunction of natural causes which rarely occurs. Some years it is too cold, other years it is too hot, some years it is too dry, others it is too wet, some soils are deficient in one respect and others fail in an opposite direction. All of these and many other diversities have to be taken into account, and on the proper appreciation of them all the result depends. More labor cannot do much, and if but little skill and capital are used, the crop will usually be small. Sometimes, however, all the elements of nature are favorable, and then just as good a crop is obtained by the poor farmer as by the good. A Texas squatter can sometimes obtain seventy bushels of wheat to the acre without much labor, merely from a conjunction of favorable circumstances. This is perhaps the extreme limit to the growth of wheat, and scientific farming has for a goal the attainment of this return on all lands every year; in other words, science would make all lands good lands.

The use of capital implies the use of more labor for a time while the obstacles to cultivation are being removed. When they are once overcome then the additional labor is no longer needed. This land can now be cultivated with as small an annual use of labor as can the land free from obstructions. The fact that a small amount of labor obtains the largest possible yield of food when the land is without obstructions to cultivation, and there is a conjunction of favorable circumstances, shows that the annual cost of cultivating all the land that should be cultivated is small. Since on some fields there is always a small cost of production, and on other fields the cost is often small, there is good ground for the belief that skill and capital can cause all improvable lands to give their best yield with no

14

more labor than is now necessary on the best lands in use.

Every increase of capital and skill reduces the quantity of labor necessary to obtain from land the present produce, and if they displace more labor than the additional labor which can be employed at a diminishing return, the return as a whole will be greater in proportion to the labor expended. If three men are displaced by skill and capital to every two additional men that can be employed, the whole number of laborers will decrease, while the produce increases. Unless the increase of labor used in agriculture was very small in proportion to the increase of capital and knowledge, the proportion of laborers engaged in agriculture to those otherwise employed could not have constantly decreased as it has done throughout modern times.

That the labor element in agriculture is nearly constant, not increasing much, if at all, when a better system is introduced, can be clearly seen when we consider what the function of labor is in the production of food. All that labor can do, to which the law of diminishing returns can be said to apply, is in the preparing of the soil. In very early stages of agricultural knowledge what labor alone could do could be as well done as now. A man with a spade and rake can prepare the land as well as any machine can do it. When machines are used, it is not because they do the work better than it can be done by manual labor, but because labor is spared. Improved processes of preparing the soil have simply found substitutes for manual labor. More labor had to be expended where fallow ploughing was customary than when this became unnecessary through use of a proper rotation of crops. The ground had to be ploughed whether a crop was raised or not, and the rotation of crops made the ground more porous and pliable. Thus less labor would prepare it as well as before, and, besides, a crop was obtained every year.

Where land is used part of the time for grazing and meadow, the reduction of labor from what was needed under the old system of agriculture is very marked. Such land need not be cultivated more than half of the time, and though half the labor is dispensed with, yet a much greater return is obtained. The rotation of crops also requires fewer laborers, as the work is scattered throughout the year and steady employment is given; the different crops being cultivated and gathered at different times, while in winter employment is given in the care of the live-stock, whereas under the old system, the return of a few days' labor had to support the laborer the entire year. So also the use of harvesting machinery causes harvesting to be done throughout the year instead of during a few days as formerly was the case, thus dispensing with

labor by giving steady work in the machine-shops. If
no other result were obtained from improved processes
than this better utilizing of labor, this result would
more than counteract any tendency there may be towards diminishing the return from agriculture.

The most important conclusion from the foregoing
facts yet remains to be noticed. It is not enough that
there is a rotation of crops, there must be a different
rotation for each variety of soil if the greatest return
for labor is to be obtained. One soil is unfitted for
wheat, another for corn, and a third for sugar-cane and
rice, the fourth for coffee or tea. Besides this, some
soils will bear a crop of wheat, or of some other article for which it is fitted, more frequently than will
other soils. Hence there must be a difference not only
in the crops for each soil, but also a difference in the
frequency in which each crop of the rotation can be
harvested with profit. For instance, some soils will
bear a crop of wheat once in three years, while on
other soils once in five or six years is as often as a crop
of wheat should be raised. A rotation should be made
of those crops which are adapted to each variety of
soil, producing each crop as frequently as the nature of
the soil will allow. Unless there is a demand for all
the different kinds of produce, and for that amount of
each article of food corresponding to the quantity of
land best fitted for its use, the best rotation of crops

cannot be utilized, and resort must be had to some other rotation less adapted to the nature of the soil on which the crops are raised. Suppose that on a given tract of land the best rotation of crops would produce one million bushels of wheat, two million bushels each of rye and oats, three million bushels of potatoes, and five million tons of grass and hay, and that the demand for food required three million bushels of wheat, one million bushels each of rye, oats, and potatoes, and three million tons of grass and hay. In this case the land must be sown to wheat more frequently than is consistent with the greatest productivity of the soil. By this change in the crops not only will the gross return from the land be reduced, but also there must be additional labor employed to produce this diminished return. The land will not be mellow and porous, and more manure and cultivation will be required than if the best rotation of crops for the land had been followed. Wherever the demand for food is such that soils unfitted for a crop are used for its production, or that a crop is raised on land more frequently than it should be used for this crop, there will be a reduction both of the gross and average return for labor on the land. This is the reason why lands in old countries require so much labor for their cultivation. The demand for food is limited to a very few articles, such as wheat or rye, potatoes, and beef, while of the other

l   14*

articles so little is desired that they cannot be produced with that frequency which is needed for the best use of the land. In most countries the demand for wheat is so great, and its price so high, that it is profitable to force its cultivation into the rotation of crops as often as possible. This can only be done by the use of much more labor than would be required for the cultivation of other crops for which the land is better fitted. Wheat is not the crop that is forced into the rotation with too great frequency in every country. In some districts it is sugar-cane, or the sugar-beet, in others it is coffee, rice, or some other crop which is in great demand. The effect, however, is the same in all these cases. Additional labor must be employed to overcome the reduced natural fertility of the soil which an unfitted rotation of crops necessitates. Just as the endeavor to raise coffee in Illinois, or oranges in Scotland, would cause a needless expenditure of labor, so a too frequent cultivation of wheat, or of some other article of food on any soil, causes a much greater outlay of labor than would be necessary if other crops were used for food to a greater extent. Suppose the demand for coffee and oranges was so great that the lands best fitted for their production could not supply the demand, and their price rose so high that their cultivation in Illinois and Scotland became profitable, could any one rightly affirm that this increase of labor proved the law of diminishing returns? If they could not, then a too great use of wheat, tobacco, or of any other article, does not prove the truth of this law. There is a great difference between the assertion that an increased demand for one or some few articles of food causes a reduced average return for labor, and the claim that the average return is diminished by an increased demand for all articles of food in that ratio for each article which will cause each tract of land to be put to the best use. The first assertion is doubtless true. It is plain that no one crop, whether wheat, rice, tobacco, or oranges, can be raised in all countries and on all soils without a great increase of the cost of production. To prove the second assertion will be a difficult task, unless the laws of nature are much different from what they now supposed to be. All the facts at present known show that both the average and the gross return gradually increases when the land is used for what it is best, and that the return is only reduced when crops which the land is not suited must be cultivated, on account of a demand for so few articles of food that a proper rotation of crops is unprofitable.

The cost of transportation is always paid out of the increased return from production on a large scale, and hence does not reduce the average return for labor. Where people are intelligent, production on a large scale will never displace local industries, unless the

average return for labor is enlarged. This increased
return arises from the combined exertion of all the
laborers. To assert that this or that portion of the
labor is less productive than some other is like main-
taining that the labor of ploughing or harrowing is
less productive than that of reaping and threshing.
Land must be ploughed and harrowed, and the crop
reaped and threshed, in order to secure a crop. It is
improper, therefore, to affirm that one portion of the
labor necessary to obtain the crop is less profitable
than some other. For the same reason it is evident
that the labor on the lands more distant from market
increases the gross returns of industry just as much as
those more favorably situated. So large a scale of
production could not be carried on without the produce of the remote lands. If this produce were not
brought to the centre of trade, the returns for all labor
would be reduced more than enough to pay for the
cost of transportation. Suppose ten million bushels
of wheat, or its equivalent in other food, were needed
at one place to produce other desired commodities on a
large scale. This amount of wheat will not be brought
to this place unless the gain from a large scale of
production will more than counterbalance the loss
through an increased cost of transportation caused by
bringing more food to one place. Under these conditions the efficiency of labor is greatest when ten

million bushels of wheat are brought to one place and the nation divided into districts each producing ten million bushels.

If the ten million bushels could be obtained nearer home without an increase of expense, certainly the average return for labor would be diminished by going so far for the food. The unused lands nearer home have enough greater cost of cultivation to counterbalance the greater cost of transportation required to obtain the food from a distance, and thus no gain can be derived by greater cultivation of the lands nearer home. The only other alternative is a decrease of the scale of production. If the district producing ten million bushels be divided into ten districts producing one million bushels, the cost of transportation will be reduced, but the scale of production must also be smaller. The loss in this way will be greater than the gain from the reduced cost of transportation, and, as a result, the average return will be no greater than before.

Suppose for a given city that the food having the greatest cost of transportation is obtained from a district at the cost of five cents a bushel, and that within the district production on a scale small enough to consume only the produce of the district could offer the producers of food ninety cents a bushel. In this case ninety-five cents a bushel must be paid for all food at the city, and this could not be done unless the larger scale of production possible in the city was productive enough to enable laborers to pay five cents more for food than could be paid by consumers in the most distant district. Unless aided by a low rate of wages and interest reducing both the gross and average return for labor, a large scale of production can displace a smaller one only when the increased productiveness is equal to the greatest cost of transportation. In any district, if the return for labor is reduced, resort will be had to the smaller scale of production. If the most distant district has the same average return as before, the nearer districts will have a greater average return. They have a smaller cost of transportation, and hence the average return for all labor is increased by the change in the scale of production and the increase in the cost of transportation. Free competition will not distribute this return equally to all persons, since there will be an increase of rent. This does not alter the façt that each laborer was necessary for so large a scale of production, and that the average return for all labor would be reduced, if any portion of the work remained unperformed, or any workmen employed on any smaller scale of production.

The diminishing returns which are claimed to attend the more complete preparation of the soil for crops by additional ploughing, harrowing, etc., are not results of natural causes. Where land requires so much preparation for tillage, either a proper rotation of crops is not carried through or the cultivators of the soil lack the capital necessary for better methods. In new countries, when the land is first tilled, a small amount of labor will prepare the soil as completely as it can be done, the land being naturally porous and mellow. It is only after years of misuse that land requires so much labor as Mill indicates to render its tillage most productive, and in the mean time the productivity of the land has rapidly fallen off. When a better system of cultivation is introduced, much labor is necessary to restore the original condition of the land. This restoration, however, being once accomplished, both the return is much increased and the labor reduced beyond what it was when the land had lost its fertility through misuse.

The land of a country is in some respects like a coalbed, which can be worked and exhausted, but it differs from a mine in that by the use of proper means its productivity can be kept up. In new countries farmers do not care for the land because it is cheap; they do not cultivate it, they work it as they would a coal-mine. Having exhausted all the natural fertility of one tract they move on to new lands, just as when an old mine is exhausted a new one is opened. So long as new land is accessible this system can be pursued, but if the soil under such a cultivation gradually loses its fertility the law of diminishing returns is not proved, even if less labor can for a time produce greater returns. If English farmers cared not for the future they could pursue the same method of agriculture that is followed in America, and for some time obtain a much greater proportional return at a much less expenditure of labor. When, however, the question is what method of cultivation will produce the greatest permanent return for the labor expended, the method ordinarily pursued in new countries must be excluded from consideration, since under it greater labor is required every year to produce the same returns, and after a time the land is completely exhausted.

If each nation were completely cut off from every other, so that it had to rely solely on its own labor to supply all its wants, the small average income of thinly-settled countries occupying only the easily cultivated land would be very apparent. It is the possibility of exchange with thickly-populated countries that makes the return for labor in new countries seem so large when compared with other countries. The comparison is not a just one, for all the manufactories employing cheap labor are in the old countries. Those laborers in the old countries who produce the articles consumed in the new countries should have their incomes averaged with those living in new countries, if a correct

average of the return for all labor from the two different modes of cultivating land is to be obtained. Suppose in England the average return of labor on the land
be kept apart from that of labor in the cities, calling
the value of the agricultural produce the return from
land and dividing this value by the number of laborers
on the land, the average return thus obtained would be
a very high one, much higher than the average return
obtained in new countries from the easily-cultivated
land. Every one will probably say that this is not a
fair way of estimating the average returns of labor
in a country, yet it is much more just than the accepted method of comparing the average returns of
old and new countries, the old countries having not
only their own non-agricultural population counted in
making up their average, but also those laborers producing for the new countries with whom they make
exchanges.

Suppose all the French factories and their employés
be removed to Belgium, would not the average income
of the remaining inhabitants be much higher than it
now is, if we accept the method now used in obtaining
the average income of the people in new countries?
It is the fallacy of this method that rent and agricultural wages are added, the sum then divided by the
number of laborers employed on the land, and the result
said to be the average return for labor. The correct

method of comparing is to take two isolated nations, the one thinly and the other thickly populated, or to consider as belonging to each nation such a part of the non-agricultural population of the whole civilized world as would correspond to its agricultural produce. From this or any other correct method it would be readily seen that the average return for all labor in newly-settled countries is much lower than the average return from those older countries where much use is made of capital to remove the obstacles to cultivation. In this case most of the land in the country can be tilled, and the advantage of a large population is obtained along with an increase of the average return for all labor.

Mill, however, asserts that a rise in price of agricultural produce is of itself sufficient evidence that the average return for labor has diminished, and in his chapter on the increase of production from land he says,—

"Now the most elementary truths of political economy show that this (the rise in price of agricultural produce) could not happen, unless the cost of production, measured in labor, of those products tended to rise. If the application of additional labor to the land was, as a general rule, attended with an increase in the proportional return, the price of produce, instead of rising, must necessarily fall as society advances. . . .

If, therefore, it be true that the tendency of agricultural produce is to rise in money price as wealth and population increase, there needs no other evidence that the labor required for raising it from the soil tends to augment when a greater quantity is demanded."

The higher price of food may indicate that there is now cultivated a lower grade of land than the poorest formerly tilled, but from this it does not follow that the average return for labor is diminished. The average return for labor depends not on the labor needed to produce the most costly portion of the produce, but on the relative quantity of the most costly and the less expensive portions. Suppose that there are four grades of land yielding for an equal amount of labor twenty, eighteen, sixteen, and fourteen bushels of wheat to the acre, and that the acres of each grade were double the number of those of the next lower grade, and that while population was increasing enough to demand the cultivation of each lower grade sufficient improvements were made so that the same labor on each grade of land could raise one more bushel to the acre. When only lands of the first class were cultivated the average return would be twenty bushels to the acre, and the price would be fixed by its cost of production. As soon, however, as population had increased so as to demand the cultivation of the second grade of land, the improvements would cause this land to yield nine-

teen bushels, and the best land would yield twenty-one
bushels to the acre. If the acres of the first class are
double the number of the second class, the average
produce of all the land will be twenty and one-third
bushels to the acre, an increase in the average return,
yet the price will be higher than before, since the cost
of production is determined by land yielding nineteen
bushels to the acre instead of twenty bushels as before.
When land of the third grade is cultivated under the
above conditions, the price will be fixed by land yielding eighteen bushels to the acre, while the average
return will be twenty and six-sevenths bushels to the
acre; and when the fourth grade of land is cultivated
the poorest land in cultivation will yield seventeen
bushels to the acre, while the average return will be
increased to twenty-one and eight-fifteenths bushels to
the acre. This illustration shows that the average
return for labor can increase along with an increase of
the price of food, and that some other evidence than
the rise in value of agricultural produce is needed to
prove that the average return for labor has diminished. This fact might be illustrated in other ways,
but these figures bring out the point needing explanation, that the average return for labor does not depend on the cost of production on the poorest land
in use, but on the relative quantity of the land of
the various grades, and that an increase of the cost of

production on some of the land does not, as claimed by Mill, counteract the beneficial effect of all improvements.

Mill's assertion that the cultivation of inferior land is in habitual antagonism to the progress of civilization, can only be maintained by showing that the tillage of the inferior lands reduces the ratio of the superior land to the inferior. The progress of civilization causes much of the poor land to become good not only through the increased use of capital and skill, but also through the gradual change in the demand for food, allowing those crops to be raised for which the land is best fitted. There are two opposing tendencies, the one causing inferior land to be cultivated, the other changing the inferior lands into good lands. The supply of inferior lands is limited, since there is a definite quantity of land, and also an ultimate limit to the productivity of each acre, the plants needing space and air in which to thrive. For these reasons the quantity of inferior land brought into cultivation must gradually decrease with the progress of civilization, and finally become exhausted. On the other hand, improvements are being made by which poor land is rapidly changed into good land, and there is no reason why most of it should not become good land, if the demand for food is so altered as to allow the best use of all land. In this way the ratio of the good to the poor land is gradually increased, and whatever increases this ratio enlarges the average return for labor.

All cultivated land may become good land, even if some land cannot be improved. The largest gross return is not obtained when all the land of a country is tilled. Forests are necessary to secure a proper supply of rain. If the amount of unimprovable land is not greater than what is needed for this purpose, it should be thus used, and all the remaining land can then be made good land. When this result is brought about, there will be no antagonism between the use of inferior land and the progress of civilization. The greatest gross return will then be obtained along with the highest average return for labor. As there will be little or no difference in the fertility of land, the price of food will be so low that rent will no longer be an important factor in the distribution of wealth.

The fact that the supply of poor land is so large that all of it cannot be used with profit for forests and other purposes not requiring cultivation, does not of itself establish the law of diminishing returns. Poor land can be cultivated only when the price of food is high, and the increase in the price of food will raise rent and lower wages. Whatever reduces wages will diminish the efficiency of labor, and if the poor land is cultivated, a less efficient class of laborers must be employed than if only good land were tilled. The use of cheap labor on the good land will reduce its fertility, and unless the amount of the produce on the poor land is greater than the amount lost by decreased efficiency of labor on the good land, the result of an effort to increase the means of subsistence by the use of the poor land and cheap labor will be a decrease instead of an increase of the food-supply.

Just as the necessity of forests to secure a proper rainfall shows that the greatest amount of food is obtainable when all the land of a country is not cultivated, so the necessity of high wages to secure efficient labor shows that there must be many apparent opportunities to increase the food-supply by means of cheap labor, which cannot be utilized without such a reduction of the intelligence and efficiency of labor as would more than counterbalance the gain obtained by the use of cheap labor.

The view of nature held by the adherents to the law of diminishing returns may be well represented by an apple-orchard, in which all the labor required is that of gathering the fruit. Some trees will bear more and better apples than others, and so long as these only are needed to supply the demand for apples, the return for labor will be high; but when more apples are needed, the reward for labor will be less, and will be continually reduced as greater and greater quantities of apples are required. As any one can pick apples, the supply will be increased as the reward for labor decreases and more of the trees are used to supply the demand. As all the work that can be done by dear labor can be performed by cheap labor, while some work that dear labor cannot perform can be done by cheap labor, the use of cheap labor in this case increases the aggregate return for labor, but lessens the average return.

If all kinds of work were like apple-picking,—the sort of labor which men performed in the original social state before capital and skill were employed,— the law of diminishing returns would doubtless be true. Fortunately for mankind, there are much easier ways of procuring food. There can be no doubt that by the use of capital and skill a greater population can be supported, and also with a greater average return for labor, than is possible in the primal social state. The question where the greater gross and average return would be found, can arise only when we compare the present social state, where the few are skilful and furnish capital for the many, who remain ignorant and unskilled, with a more advanced state of society where each laborer is skilful and saves for himself. In considering the gross produce of these two social states, those living in the advanced state would be debarred from all opportunities to labor where the return was small, while those living in the present social state would lose where the return was high, inefficient labor not producing as much as the skilled but dearer labor which might be employed wherever the return for labor was sufficient to remunerate it. Which of the two social states could produce the greater gross return would depend upon the relation of the good lands to the poor. If most of the land is or can be made good, the skilled laborers of the more advanced state of society could produce a greater gross return than cheap labor and still obtain a high reward for their labor. On the other hand, most of the land being poor, cheap labor would have a field of employment so large that it could produce a greater gross return than skilled labor, even if it were less efficient, on the few good acres which society possesses.

To illustrate, let us suppose that in a given country one million men can be employed in cultivating the land, each man producing two hundred bushels of wheat, while on the land not tilled each man could produce but one hundred bushels; and, further, that if the wages of the laborers were reduced one-half, so that the inferior land might be cultivated, their efficiency would be reduced ten per cent. If this be true, the effect of the cultivation of the inferior lands on the gross return would depend upon the quantity of the inferior land. The reduction of the wages of the laborers employed on the superior land would according to this supposition lessen the return from their

m

labor ten per cent., or from two hundred million to one hundred and eighty million. If the quantity of the inferior land were sufficient to employ two hundred thousand men, they would produce, at one hundred bushels each, twenty million bushels, and the gross produce of all the land would be just equal to what the superior lands alone produced before the inferior land was tilled. Were the quantity of inferior land smaller, so that only one hundred thousand men could be employed on it, they would produce but ten million bushels, and the gross return would be lowered to one hundred and ninety million bushels, a loss of ten million bushels. On the other hand, if three hundred thousand men could find work on the inferior land, they would produce thirty million bushels, and the gross return would be increased by ten million bushels.

From this illustration it is evident that the quantitative relation of inferior to superior lands determines whether or not the gross return will be increased by the cultivation of both. If the quantity of inferior lands be relatively large, their cultivation will increase the gross return and lower the average return. When, however, the quantity of inferior lands is relatively small, their tillage will reduce both the gross and average return for labor.

It has been shown in the previous discussion that in

a society in which all are skilled and possess capital, most of the land becomes good land. If this be true in such a society, both the gross and average returns are much greater than in the present social state where so much use is made of cheap labor.

The alternatives between which a society must choose are less labor and a greater gross and average return on the one hand, and more labor and a smaller gross and average return on the other. The third alternative which the law of diminishing returns implies—a greater gross and a less average return—is an impossibility where the greater part of the land of a country is good. It overlooks the necessity of high wages and high interest to induce all to save and become skilful, the gross return being lessened unless all do this.

The effect of social progress in increasing both the gross and average returns may be represented by supposing a series of islands of equal size arranged in a line north and south, each island being more fertile and productive than its northern neighbor. The islands lying to the south would support a greater population and with a greater average return than those to the north, more food being raised and at less proportional cost. If only the one farthest north were inhabited and the rest unknown, population would increase there until it would be so great that the average return to labor would be lessened. Suppose at this juncture that the island next south is discovered, and that the inhabitants of the first island, rather than have their incomes reduced, remove bodily to the new island, which can support a larger population and give a greater average return to their labor. The population still increasing, finally becomes so great that the average return again begins to decline. Then let the third island be discovered and all the people transfer themselves to it, thereby more than regaining the old average return for their labor. So long as new islands can be discovered, this process can be repeated, and at each removal both the number of the population and their average income would be augmented. To make this illustration applicable to our purpose we must further suppose that to the occupancy of each island the condition is attached that if the inhabitants allow a reduction in the average return to their labor, they must leave the island and return to the one whence they came. In this case all those resources which allow an increase of population, but require a decrease of the average return, could not be utilized, and when, on each island, population is increased to the point where the average return begins to decline, the increase must be stopped, a new island discovered, or the people must return to the island to the north, where both the population and the average produce of labor have been reduced.

Granting these suppositions, a greater population would always be in conjunction with a greater average return. There would be but one island in the series where people of a given average income could live, and if the incomes of these people were less than that of the people of another island, the population would also be less.

I contend that there are such conditions offered by the different social states through which each progressive society passes. If a greater population is supported, the average income is increased, and if 'the income is lowered, society finds itself forced back into a lower social state, where its numbers are also reduced. Each new social state imposes some new condition, which can only be complied with so long as the average return is greater than before. The people must gradually learn to work regularly, cease to wage war, respect property, accumulate capital, demand for food what nature is best fitted to supply; and, lastly, they must be intelligent and skilled workmen, each saving for himself. As these conditions are complied with, both population and the average return are increased; if they are violated, both the population and the average return are reduced. This is especially true of the last condition, as a person will acquire skill and save only as he can thereby better his condition. A society all of whose members are skilled, each one saving for himself, can

16

support a larger population than any other and at a greater average income. If this high return for labor is not maintained, skill will be lost and capital decreased, and only a smaller population will be able to find support, and at a lower rate of return for labor.

If the foregoing facts are brought into their proper relation, they will demonstrate the correctness of the position that the law of agricultural returns is a law of limited not of diminishing returns. Up to a certain point, depending on the knowledge and skill of the inhabitants, the return increases in proportion to the labor expended; beyond that point no return can be had without an increase of knowledge and capital, or without a change in the demand for food, by which the qualities of the land are brought into better use.

It is only during an early stage of civilization that the law of diminishing returns is true. Then but small use is made of skill and capital, and there is a demand only for a few articles of food. To a nation that relies solely on manual labor to supply its wants, only the easily cultivated land has a small cost of production, and as population increases soils must be cultivated that are less productive of the few articles of food which are in demand. Only a small proportion of the land is good land, and hence the increase of population is detrimental to the average return for labor. With the progress of civilization the ratio of the good land to the poor is increased, and the disadvantage of an increasing population is gradually diminished, until at length the ratio of the good to the poor land is so great that the advantages of a large population more than counterbalance the disadvantages. When, finally, each man becomes skilled and saves for himself, and all persons so adjust their demands for food to the natural conditions by which they are surrounded that all the land may be used for what it is best fitted, the average return for labor will increase with the growth of population, and the greatest possible population can be supported with a much larger average return for labor than can be obtained when the number of people is more limited.

CHAPTER VII.

FREE-TRADE.

IN the previous chapters we have already considered the leading principle by which the advantages of free-trade between different nations must be determined. It has been shown that a combination of cheap labor and low interest will produce an approximation of the values of food and raw material to that of manufactured commodities. The power of underselling arises from a false economy of skilled labor; as cheap labor gradually displaces the skilled, the price of finished articles falls and that of food and raw material is increased. If cheap labor and low interest in domestic commerce produce an approximation of prices, displacing skilled labor, the same result will be brought about by free foreign exchange, and manufactured commodities will be produced by the nation which, having the lowest rate of wages and interest, can create the greatest approximation of the price of food to that of finished commodities.

There are good reasons for regarding this the most important principle determining the advantages of foreign exchange. It is true that there are great varictics of soil and climate throughout the earth, each peculiarly fitted for some particular products, yet the demand for food is practically limited to a few articles, and if a nation wishes to exchange any considerable amount of produce with other nations, these articles must be exported, no matter how much advantage it may have in other articles. Take the trade of England and India for example. India, doubtless, has important advantages over England in the production of rice and other tropical articles of food. The demand for food of this nature in England is very limited, as the main articles of English diet are wheat-bread and beef, and if India wants English commodities to any extent, wheat or beef must be sent in exchange. As a result we see the land of India used to produce wheat to send to England instead of rice, the article for which the land is particularly adapted, so that the productive power of India is reduced to but a small fraction of what it would otherwise be. As another example take the case of Ireland. It is well known that the land of Ireland is extremely well fitted for potatoes, yet as the demand for food in England is not for potatoes, but for beef, the land of Ireland must be used for grazing purposes, and the country is thereby almost depopulated. So long as the English demand only wheat and beef the land of every nation trading with them must be used for raising wheat and cattle, no

16*

matter what may be the advantages which they possess for producing other articles of food. The fact which I wish to bring into prominence is not that exchange with England is disadvantageous, but that foreign trade is of little importance to any nation so long as the demand for food is limited to a few articles. Of what utility is it to one nation that its land will produce excellent rye, potatoes, rice, and other similar products so long as the nations with which it trades have little or no demand for them? If the list of imports of any civilized nation be examined, it will be seen that nine-tenths, or more, of all the imports are manufactured commodities and a few articles for food and clothing which can be produced anywhere. Sugar, tobacco, and cotton are the only articles from semitropical regions which are desired in any considerable quantities, and if more lands in these regions are cultivated than will supply the very limited demand for these articles, crops better fitted to temperate climates must be produced.

Certainly the waste of labor is as great when plants best fitted for the temperate zone are produced in the tropical zone as when tropical plants are raised in temperate regions. An orange can, it is said, be produced in Portugal with half the labor that is required in France, and when the French exclude the oranges from Portugal they double the amount of labor which would otherwise be needed to procure an orange. That this is true I have no desire to deny, but it is easy to show that a free-trade policy also causes a like waste of labor and to a much greater extent. Suppose the demand for more oranges were so great that in Portugal and elsewhere the land best fitted for oranges could not supply the demand, and the price of oranges rose so high that they could be raised with profit in France. The land in France would be used for orange-groves only when all the various grades of land, from the best of Portugal to the French land most productive of oranges, have been diverted from their most productive use and devoted to the production of oranges. Now the objection urged by free-traders against a duty on oranges is that the labor employed in orange-groves would be diverted from the other industries, where it is most productive. An undue demand for oranges would have the same effect. When the price of oranges is high, most of the land producing them is more productive of other articles of food. The very same fields of France whose use for orange-groves caused so much complaint on the part of the free-traders when the tariff raised the price of oranges, are now used for their production. The greater demand for oranges certainly does not increase the fitness of French soil for orange-groves. If there is a reduced return for labor when a tariff causes the land of France to be used to produce oranges, there is a still greater reduction of the efficiency of labor when this result is brought about by the increase of the demand for oranges. The increased demand will cause not only the land of France to be used for a purpose for which it is poorly fitted, but also large tracts of land in other countries less productive of oranges than the land of Portugal would be turned into orange-groves.

If an examination be made to discover how much land is diverted from its best use by a free-trade policy, it will be seen that the waste of labor which it causes greatly exceeds that resulting from an opposite policy. When a French tariff causes a few acres in France to be used for the production of oranges a great outcry is raised at the waste of labor, but when free-trade causes the land of India to be used for the production of wheat, no free-trader notices the waste of labor. Yet in this manner the productivity of the land of India is more reduced than is the land of France when used for orange-groves. A free-trade policy causes the land of the whole world to be used for the production of a few articles like wheat, and of no few articles will land yield as much as if all that variety of food were desired which would cause each acre to be used most efficiently.

There are several good reasons why a free-trade

policy will divert the land of exchanging countries
from its best use. Most articles of food have great
bulk and weight. When they are carried to a great
distance, the cost of transportation is so great that
they become more costly to the consumers in distant
lands than are the other articles of food, which,
though supplied by nature less abundantly, can be
transported with but little expense. Many articles
of food cannot be preserved, and must be consumed
at the place where they are produced. They can be
utilized only by a people living where they are abundant, and are of no more use to distant lands than are
the mines of an uninhabited country. If fruits and
other perishable commodities could be as easily preserved and transported as wheat can be, the whole
economic history of the world would have been very
different from what it has been. The food of every
nation would be other than it is, while the advantages
of free-traders would be greatly increased. It is, however, of no importance to the world that there are
many kinds of food in other climates so long as the
cost of transporting them is more of a hinderance to
obtaining them than the worst tariff would be. Even
of the articles of food that can be transported, some can
endure transportation better than others. Corn, for
example, is much more liable to damage than wheat,
and hence for cities distant from the centres of produc-

tion wheat will be less costly as a means of support than corn, the reverse of what is true in an adjacent market. In this way a foreign demand, offering a premium for the production of those articles of food best fitted for transportation, diverts land from its best use, and by reducing the efficiency of labor, produces that very result against which free-traders so strenuously object when it is occasioned by a protective tariff.

The most important misuse of land, however, arises from the habits of that class of laborers which survive when a nation steadily adheres to a free-trade policy. Only by an extended use of production on a large scale, accompanied by cheap labor and low interest, can so great an approximation of prices be brought about in one nation as to displace the industrial classes in other nations where the habits of the laborers are of such a nature that they are inclined to save for themselves. To produce a great approximation of prices there must be on the part of most laborers a demand for those articles of food and drink which create in the consumers the strongest appetite and the greatest desire for consumption of food as a source of pleasure. By their use the thought of future welfare is displaced by the desire for immediate enjoyment, and the cravings of an abnormal appetite lead its possessor to work for less wages than will those who desire less exclusive pleasures. If soup or coffee created a stronger appetite than beer or whiskey, and rye-bread and rice were more palatable than wheat-bread and meat, the industrial centres of the world would be differently located from where they now are, and the land of every country would be used for producing a very different class of articles of food. As it now is, the stimulating food and drink demanded by a low class of laborers cause most of the land to be used for what it is poorly fitted, and free-trade, by assisting the survival of those laborers having the strongest appetites, reduces the efficiency of labor more than could be done even by a prohibitory tariff, which cuts off each nation from the advantages of soil and climate possessed by other nations.

When a much higher civilization has displaced the present, and the nations of the earth, using a much more varied and less stimulating diet, conform to the natural conditions by which they are surrounded, foreign exchange will be of great importance to them. So long, however, as the demand for food is limited to a few articles, differences of soil and climate are of little moment. The controlling circumstances in foreign as well as domestic exchange are the rates of wages and interest. Just as in domestic trade the class offering the highest price for food survive, so in foreign trade one nation can displace the producers of manu-

factured commodities in other nations by causing so
great an approximation of the price of food to finished commodities that it will be more profitable for
producers of food in other nations to exchange with it
than with home producers. As, however, the advocates of free-trade deny this fact and claim that free-
trade is always advantageous to both exchanging
nations, it is necessary to examine the arguments by
which they seek to establish their position.

One of Adam Smith's favorite arguments is that it
is good policy in a family to sell in the dearest and
buy in the cheapest market, and that what is good
policy for a family cannot be a poor policy for a nation.
In this argument he overlooks the important difference
between a family and a nation. In a family the distribution is or ought to be according to the needs of
the different members, or according to the part taken
by each in production. In a nation this is not the case.
Each class has its own interests and desires, and looks
out for them alone, and is perfectly willing to sacrifice
the interests of others to its own welfare. If rent rises
and wages and interest fall, landlords do not share their
extra gains with the other classes, nor do either of the
other classes relinquish a profit or share it with the
others. Nations are not families, at least nations where
competition exists. Adam Smith's argument would
hold good in a commune where the share of each per-

son was given according to any plan which allowed none to be merely landlord, capitalist, or laborer, the division of produce taking place, as it does in a family, according to some maxim of justice.

Free competition spoils all this, and compels the people of nations to act in a way different from that they would follow if they were a family or commune; and nothing can be known of the effect of a measure until it is determined what effect it will have on the distribution of wealth.

When one of the exchanged products is an article of food or a product of mines, the exchange becomes disadvantageous to the country exporting this produce, since the additional quantity needed for export can under present conditions be obtained only at an increased proportional cost, and the gain in the exchange will be counteracted by the increased cost at which the additional supply is produced.

The capitalists and laborers lose not only on the amount exported, but on all produce, as there is only one price for an article in the same market, and hence the demand for export raises the price not only of the part sent abroad but of all that consumed at home. Since only a small part is ever sent abroad, the gains of the landlords from this part are only a small fraction of the gains which the increase in price enables them to obtain from the capitalists and laborers, who are

I   *n*   17

compelled to purchase all their food at the augmented price.

It may be objected that if the nation as a whole lose more than it gains the exchange would not take place. This would be a valid objection if there were no separate classes in the country, and the loss fell on the same persons who make the gain. Those who make the gain, however, are the landlords, while the losses fall either on the capitalists or on the laborers or on both.

Economists often call attention to the absurdities of general high prices, but they usually fail to perceive that the same absurdity is involved in general low prices. To reduce the value of one article raises the value of that for which it is exchanged just as much as raising the value of one commodity decreases the value of the commodities for which it is given. If, then, it is desirable to discover what are the permanent effects of a change in foreign trade, it can be done only by examining what articles are lowered and what are raised in value. Other methods will give us only the temporary effects which accompany the change, without revealing anything of the final results which are sure to follow.

If two countries are thrown into commercial relations, in one of which food is cheaper than in the other, all the laborers and capitalists in the former (where food is cheap) will lose, while the same classes in the other country will correspondingly gain. The opposite, however, will be the effect in the case of the landlords, since in the first rents will rise, while in the second they will fall to a like degree. With free-trade existing between England and America, the price of food in both nations must be nearly the same, and would be just the same but for the cost of transportation. The price of food is raised in America and lowered in England. At the same time in America manufactured goods fall, while in England they rise. This would be advantageous to English capitalists and laborers, and to a like degree disadvantageous to those of America, while American landlords would gain at the expense of the same class in England.

It may, however, be urged that American capitalists can avoid this fall of wages by occupying new lands and becoming landlords and farmers themselves. In a very new country this can be done, often without much loss, but the older the country becomes the more difficult is the change, and when the lands are once occupied it is impossible.

A favorite argument of the free-traders is that under a system of free-trade the same amount of capital and labor is employed as under a system of protection, and in a more efficient manner. When we buy we also sell, and we must use the product of home labor to buy foreign goods, and hence, it is claimed, when goods are purchased on a foreign market as much home labor and capital are employed as before, while they are used more efficiently. As soon as rent is paid in a country a given value of food does not contain the same quantity of labor as the manufactured commodities for which it is exchanged. If a farmer sells two thousand dollars' worth of corn and pays six hundred dollars rent, the product only contains fourteen hundred dollars of wages and profit; hence where a change is made by which food is exported instead of manufactured articles, much less labor and capital are employed, as much less as the amount of the rent.

Whenever an article is purchased in a foreign market, it is true that a domestic product must be given in exchange for it, but that does not prove that the home labor market has not thereby suffered a contraction. Suppose silk for the English market had been purchased in France, and English cutlery be sent to France in exchange. If now the silk should be manufactured in England and exchanged for the cutlery, the demand for cutlery would not be reduced, nor would the demand for any other article decrease. The demand for food would increase to supply the additional labor employed by the silk-producers, and they would have the cutlery, before exported, with which to purchase the needed food. In France, on the other hand, the demand for silk would be reduced by the value of the cutlery formerly imported, and there would be a quantity of food of equal value, formerly consumed by the silk laborers in France, for which there would be no demand, the laborers now having no cutlery to exchange for the food. There being in France a surplus of food, and in England a surplus of cutlery of equal value, these would be exchanged for one another. The result of the exchange would be, English cutlery would go to France as before, while food would be sent to England to pay for it instead of silk. The demand for labor in England would be increased by the number employed by the silk-producers, while to a like amount would the demand for labor in France decline.

A demand for a product of home industry gives its producers the same power to purchase goods in a foreign market as those with whom they exchange previously had, and foreign commerce does not thereby decline unless the producers of the commodity buy food which was formerly exported. In any other case the same articles will be exported as before, and food imported instead of the commodity now manufactured at home.

The most familiar argument used to support free-trade is the doctrine of comparative cost, which was first expounded by Ricardo, and has ever since been accepted as the corner-stone of the free-trade position.

This doctrine asserts that the exchange of commodities in foreign commerce is not determined by the absolute cost of production, but by the difference in the comparative cost.

If one of two countries has the advantage in production in all respects, and to the same degree, there would be, it is claimed, no exchange of commodities; but if the advantages be greater in some commodities than in others, an exchange would take place.

Let me illustrate by a familiar example. If as much cloth can be produced in Poland for one hundred days' labor as can be produced in England by one hundred and fifty days' labor, while the corn which is produced in Poland by one hundred days' labor cannot be produced in England short of two hundred days' labor, a sufficient motive for exchange would exist. With the quantity of cloth produced in England for one hundred and fifty days' labor England could purchase as much corn as was produced in Poland for one hundred days' labor, which would be as great a quantity as could be produced in England by two hundred days' labor. By importing corn from Poland, and paying for it with cloth, England would obtain for one hundred and fifty days' labor what would otherwise cost her two hundred days' labor.

The fallacy in this argument lies in the erroneous conception of the cost of production, by which the effect of rent is disregarded. Rent, we are told, is not an element of the cost of production, the cost being measured solely by the number of days' labor and abstinence required to produce a commodity. In other words, the cost of production is held to be affected only by wages and profits.

Now, rent does not affect the cost of production in the sense that it makes general high or low prices, but neither do wages nor profits. High wages or profits do not make general high prices; they affect prices only inasmuch as different articles have, as elements of their cost, wages and profits in different proportions. If in the cost of one article wages enter as an element of cost more largely than in another article, the first will rise and fall in value as wages rise and fall, while the value of the second will change in an opposite direction. It is in this way that rent affects the cost of production.

As rent increases, those articles in whose value rent enters more largely will rise in price, while others in which rent enters to a less degree will fall in value.

Agricultural products are, of course, those into the price of which rent enters most largely, and these will rise in value as rent rises; they are, therefore, the articles which it is least advantageous to produce at home and most advantageous to import from abroad. This argument, put in the terminology of Ricardo and Mill, is as follows: The cost of production is measured by the number of days' labor and abstinence. But the number of days' labor required to produce a given quantity of food depends upon the amount required for consumption. The greater the gross quantity required the larger the quantity of labor which must be used to produce each part of it, and hence, with every increase in the demand for food, its price will rise and that of manufactured articles will fall. Labor and capital are as efficient as formerly in all manufactured articles, but less efficient in the production of food. Since, according to the doctrine of comparative cost, those articles of commerce in which the country's labor is most efficiently employed are exported, and those in which the labor is least efficient are imported, food will now be imported and manufactured goods exported. Whether or not rent is admitted as an element of the cost of production makes no difference in the argument if the fact is kept in view that the cost of production of food increases, and the efficiency of the labor used in its production decreases, as the pressure of population becomes greater. This reveals why profits do not rise when wages fall, why the character of the external trade changes when wages and profits fall, and why the comparative quantity of labor required for the production of different commodities changes as population increases.

Let us suppose, as does Mill, that one hundred days' labor in producing either cloth or corn would yield as much in Poland as one hundred and fifty days' labor in England. In that case, of course, no trade would follow, but if rent should rise in one country and not in the other, exchange would become profitable. If rent in England should increase through the demand for more food, so that the corn which could be produced in Poland for one hundred days' labor now requires one hundred and sixty days' labor in England, as would be the case when rent equalled ten days' labor, the trade would be profitable, since now the return of one hundred and fifty days' labor in cloth, if taken to Poland, will exchange for the product of one hundred days' labor in corn,—an amount equal to that obtained in England by one hundred and sixty days' labor,—ten days' labor would be saved, overlooking the cost of transportation to illustrate the underlying principle.

But what would be the effect in Poland? Either profits and wages there must fall, or all the food will be shipped to England, and if they fall enough so that the rent in Poland is equal to that in England, the trade will again cease. If rent should again rise in England through the cultivation of poorer land, so that it requires one hundred and seventy days' labor to procure the amount of food formerly produced in one hundred and fifty days, trade with Poland would again be profitable, for the comparative cost would be again favorable to exchange, and Polish capitalists and laborers would again be compelled to give up another portion of their profits and wages or let the food be exported to England.

In this case we supposed that rent rose in England, which was naturally at a disadvantage both in corn and cloth; but the same effects would take place if rent should rise in Poland, for England would now be compelled to pay a like rent or have its food shipped to Poland. For if rent rose in Poland so that the corn formerly produced in one hundred days now cost one hundred and ten days' labor, and the product of one hundred days' labor in cloth be taken to England, it will exchange for the product of one hundred and fifty days' labor in corn; this, when brought back to Poland, would be the amount obtained there for one hundred and ten days' labor. Hence the trade would be profitable, and would continue until the English wages and profits were so reduced that they could pay a rent equal to the rent of Poland, when exchange would again cease, unless a subsequent rise of rent in Poland should again make trade profitable and cause further reductions of profits and wages in England.

The foregoing illustrations show the effect of rent on foreign trade when one of the exchanged commodities is an article of the food-supply, but the effect is just as marked when both the exchanged articles are manufactured commodities. If it costs eighty dollars to make in France a quantity of silk which in England costs one hundred and twenty dollars, and if it costs ninety-six dollars in France to make a quantity of cloth which in England is made at a cost of one hundred dollars, then, according to the doctrine of comparative cost, it will be profitable for the French to buy cloth of the English and for the English to buy silk of the French, although France has an advantage in the production of both silk and cotton. This would be true provided there was nothing but cloth in England which the French wanted and nothing but silk in France desired by the English; that is, so long as the trade is confined to cloth and silk it would be profitable and advantageous.

There is, however, an important element omitted, one which changes the entire outlook of the case. There is a class of articles which are always in demand in France, England, and in all other countries, namely, articles of food. A bushel of wheat or a bag of potatoes is just as useful in one country as in another. Agricultural produce can always be used to procure foreign goods, to settle any balance of trade, and is the usual method by which the balance of trade is settled. Before any determination of the profit or loss in any exchange can be made, the price of food must always be brought into consideration, as with any of the articles of food the balance can be settled and the course of trade changed. To determine in our illustration what would be the course of the exchange, we must first determine the price of food in both countries. The result of this investigation will decide what will be the result of the exchange. Either the price of food in England is lower than that of France, equal to it, or dearer. If the price in England is lower than that in France, or equal to it, all the cloth and silk of both countries will be manufactured in France. Overlooking the cost of transportation, no one in England will pay one hundred dollars for a quantity of cloth when he can get it by sending ninety-six dollars' worth of wheat to France, and still less will any one pay one hundred and twenty dollars for silk in England when eighty dollars' worth of wheat will buy it in France. So long, then, as the price of food is not greater in England than in France, the manufacture of both silk and cloth in England will be impossible, and all of both articles needed in England will be obtained from France, food being given in exchange.

If, however, the price of food in England is higher than in France, the course of trade will be changed. Suppose the quantity of food requisite to procure ninety-six dollars' worth of cloth in France were worth one hundred and five dollars in England. In this case all the cloth would be manufactured in England both for France and England, although according to our supposition the same labor in France will produce four dollars' worth of cloth more than in England. For no one in France will give ninety-six dollars for a given quantity of cloth if this money invested in food will sell for one hundred and five dollars in England, and with one hundred dollars of this he can purchase the amount of cloth for which he would have to give ninety-six dollars in France, as by the exchange with England he could save five dollars. If, again, the price of food in England were still higher, so that the quantity of food worth eighty dollars in France cost one hundred and twenty-five dollars in England, neither cloth nor silk would be manufactured in France, although the same labor in France will produce forty dollars' worth of silk more than in England. Food costing eighty dollars in France would bring one hundred and twenty-five dollars in England, and by expending one hundred and twenty dollars there, the same quantity of silk could be obtained which would cost eighty dollars in France; that is, by sending food to England and importing cloth and silk a profit could be made, although the labor of France had according to our supposition a decided advantage in the production of both commodities.

18

The difference between the prices of raw material and food and those of finished commodities determines the rate of wages and interest. If in one country this difference is small, all countries which exchange with it will be forced to reduce their wages and profits to its rates or lose their food-supply and other raw material.

Suppose that in all countries but one, fifteen yards of calico or three yards of woollen cloth exchanged for a bushel of wheat, and that in the remaining country twenty yards of calico or four yards of woollen cloth exchanged for a bushel of wheat. As calico, woollen cloth, and other like articles can be produced in any quantity demanded, this one nation could produce enough of these to supply all the other nations, and as it offers better terms to the owners of wheat than do the home-producers of cloth and calico, it would obtain all the wheat raised in the various countries so long as the home-producers of cloth and calico demanded a ratio of exchange less favorable to landlords than that offered by the nation having cheap labor and low interest. Food will not have two values in the same market, but will all go to those who offer the highest price, if no legal obstacle is placed in the way. It is only by duties placed upon the export of wheat, or on the importation of cloth, that fifteen yards of calico or three yards of woollen cloth can be made to exchange for a bushel of wheat, if for this bushel a foreign nation offers twenty yards of calico or four yards of woollen cloth.

So long as foreign trade is profitable, each nation to a great degree has it in its power to determine what shall be the ratio of exchange between raw materials and manufactured commodities. When England adopted a free-trade policy she did it to change the ratio of exchange, so that more food should exchange for a smaller quantity of manufactured articles. The importation of food lowered its price, reduced rent, and raised wages and profits. This even free-traders can see, but what they fail to perceive is that the opposite of this must be the effect on the other nations exporting food. In these countries the price of food and rent will be raised, and wages and profits will decline to a like amount.

The income of a farmer is derived partially from rent and partially from the labor and capital which he employs. A rise in the price of agricultural produce increases his income from rent, but reduces that derived from labor and capital, and the amount of his gain above his loss will be indicated by the rise in the price of his land. If free-trade is adopted, the price of land will be high and wages and interest low, and the owners of land will have all the profit arising from the high price of food. This does not show, however, that the farmers as a class will be benefited, since they are usually not the real owners of the soil in countries where land has a high price. The real farmers suffer along with the other classes, as their wages and profits are determined by the same circumstances, while those who gain by the high price of land may live wherever they choose, and this will usually be far away from the places from which they draw their income.

The welfare and prosperity of every nation demands that the value of food and other raw material should be as low as possible in comparison to that of other commodities, the whole value of which is made up of wages and profits. The policy which will bring this about is the best one for a nation to follow. I do not wish to assert that it is never desirable that the value of food or other raw material should be raised at the expense of wages and profits. Such a policy will often produce good results, if the view which I have advanced elsewhere of the causes and conditions of rent is correct. A high price of food is often necessary to induce men to overcome those obstacles which cause most of the land of a country to remain in a poor state of cultivation or not to be cultivated at all. The land must be drained, forests and other obstacles must be removed, and this will only be done when the value of food is high. When these obstacles are once removed, the price of food may fall without the supply being decreased. The same is true of mines. There are many expenses involved in the opening of mines which will only be incurred when the value of mineral products is high; but, as in the case of the food-supply, when mining industries are once placed in a prosperous condition, the supply of mineral products will not be reduced even if there should be a great reduction in their value. It should, however, always be kept in mind that such bounties to land-owners, whether in the form of free-trade, when the foreign price is higher than the domestic, or of protection, when the foreign price is the lower, are at the expense of wages and profits, and should be discontinued as soon as possible, so that the value of food and other raw material may be low in comparison to other commodities. To accomplish this result duties either on the exportation of food or on the importation of manufactured commodities will be necessary so long as any foreign nation will offer more for food or other raw material than would be offered by domestic producers if there were no foreign demand.

These illustrations show that we cannot determine the character of foreign trade by considering alone the efficiency of labor in the different countries, as the result is conditioned by the price of food, and until this is known nothing can be determined as to the course of exchange. Everything may be manufactured at a point where the labor of the world is most inefficient, if at that point the pressure of the demand for food is so great as to cause its price to be higher there than elsewhere. The increase of rent disturbs the natural course of commerce and forces upon each nation as unequal a distribution of wealth as that of the nation which suffers most from this cause. A nation has only one means to protect its people from the high price of food caused by the unequal distribution of wealth in a neighboring nation, and that is by duties levied either on the importation of commodities or on the exportation of food. If neither of those means are resorted to, nothing can prevent such an approximation of the value of food and other raw material to the value of manufactured commodities as will produce a low rate of wages.

CHAPTER VIII.

THE MEANS OF MAINTAINING A HIGH STANDARD OF LIFE.

IT has long been a current maxim that the use of cheap food is destructive of a high standard of life, and keeping in mind the facts proven in the preceding chapters, it is easy to see why such an opinion should be prevalent. The cheap kinds of food are those whose production requires the least skill and capital, and hence a lower class of labor is employed than is possible where more intelligence is requisite. Wherever nature does much and man but little, a low class of laborers can accomplish all that is to be done. The more intelligent classes, as the price of food rises above what they can pay, gradually disappear, leaving society made up of two distinct classes, the very rich and powerful on the one hand, the poor and oppressed on the other.

What makes the difference, for instance, between England and Egypt lies in the fact that in England the obstacles to be overcome are so great that a much higher class of labor must be employed than is the case in Egypt, where nature, by means of the river Nile, keeps up the fertility of the land and allows methods of cultivation to be employed which would ruin England in a few years. In all warm countries, such as India, Cuba, and Mexico, little clothing is required, food is cheap and abundant, and nature does so much that little or nothing is required of man but to gather the food which nature has prepared. As there are no obstacles to be overcome, the lowest classes of men survive and displace their betters.

The effect on the standard of life of a lack of obstacles to be overcome is plainly visible in the Southern States of the Union as compared with the Northern States. If a low class of labor in the North by the use of the hoe and other rude implements could have produced as great a surplus above the cost of production as is the case in Southern States, slaves would have been employed in the North as well as in the South, and the economic condition of the North would have been no better than that of the South. What saved the North was the fact that slaves and other low classes of labor were not profitable. Thus laboring men with a much higher standard of life were allowed to survive in the North than would have been the case had the obstacles been fewer and less difficult to surmount.

The same condition of things can be observed in all

parts of the world. Wherever the obstacles are few the people are low and ignorant, while as the obstacles increase the inhabitants become more intelligent, since the more ignorant and inefficient classes cannot survive. Different societies and different classes in the same society can be correctly graded by the difficulties which stand in the way of making a living requiring skill, intelligence, and capital to overcome. If little or no skill and capital are required in a country, the people will be ignorant and depraved, and lack the energy and other qualities necessary to cause a high civilization. It is only where the means of supporting a low class of population are absent that the higher and more intelligent classes are able to displace their inferiors. Wherever game or fish is plenty, or cheap food is obtainable, as potatoes in Ireland or rice in India, there is sure to be found a low class of inhabitants. None of these means of support offers any obstacles which cannot be overcome by the lowest classes of society, and the intelligent and skilful, having no advantage in the conflict for life, either disappear or sink to the level of their inferiors.

The intelligence and enterprise of any society depends upon the relative numbers of the occupations requiring skill and capital to those which require little or none of these requisites for their successful prosecution. If in but few places skill and capital are required, while the mass of the people can exist without them, then a low civilization is a necessary consequence. On the other hand, if the greater part of the population must be intelligent and save capital, a high civilization will be the result. Whatever can be done by cheap labor is always done by it, and the intelligent classes are confined to those occupations which require so much skill that the lower classes, not being able to perform the work, are shut out from competition.

For these reasons, a high civilization has been developed only in countries where the obstacles were so great that only the more intelligent could survive. Even here it is insecure, as the obstacles decrease as the country advances in civilization. Every improvement makes it possible for a lower class to survive, and progress is retarded and often completely stopped by the relative increase of the lower classes, which the removing of obstacles, insurmountable to them alone, has made possible. When land is once cleared of woods and drained, and stones and other like hinderances to cultivation removed, succeeding generations do not have to do these things over again, and a class of laborers come in which lack the energy that was necessary to overcome the difficulties to be found in all new countries.

Production upon a large scale and the use of machinery have the same detrimental effect, for the pro-

This follows from his position on the law of limited returns; and it is as true as the law of diminishing returns here the force of his contention is minimized.

portion of the intelligent to the unintelligent is greatly lessened by their use. All the capital in large establishments being furnished by a few persons, and all the intelligence by a few skilled mechanics and foremen, all the work can be performed by a very low class of laborers, who drive out the skilled and intelligent by the low price at which they offer their services.

The reduction of the cost of transportation and the increase of commerce operate in a like manner, as they allow a class of laborers who have not energy enough to immigrate, to ship the produce of their labor so cheaply to the new countries as to lessen the return which the laborers of these countries would otherwise obtain for their labor. At the same time the low rates of passage to the new countries cause the immigrants to be of a much lower grade of intelligence than they would otherwise be if commerce had more obstacles to encounter.

Every improvement has the same effect as if the country were removed farther south to a place where less energy was required of its inhabitants, and if progress, as it is likely to do, keeps on in the same direction as in the past, all the present civilized nations will soon be in a position similar to that occupied by Egypt and India, and the difficulties of keeping up a high civilization will be as great as they are in these hot countries. The proportion of the occupations requiring intelligence as a condition of success in all civilized nations is constantly decreasing, and may in time become as small as it now is in either Egypt or India.

If these facts be true, we cannot rely on natural causes to protect us from the evils arising from ignorance. These evils, assisted by free competition, operate against the intelligent and aid the success of cheap labor when combined with low interest. Unless as the natural obstacles which prevent the survival of the ignorant are lessened, social obstacles which have a like effect are put in their places, we cannot but expect that the low and ignorant will gradually displace the intelligent, until at length civilization itself will be destroyed by decrease of those classes which sustain it.

Just as the dam which, by obstructing the free passage of the water and furnishing the power by which the mill is propelled, is gradually destroyed by the force of the water and the level of the water lowered so that at length the water has not power to turn the mill, so progress and improvements diminish the force of civilization by reducing the obstacles which prevent the survival of the ignorant until civilization loses all its force.

We would not think of permitting the level of the mill-pond to be lowered, nor of forbidding repairs because natural causes had lowered it; nor should we permit the fact that progress is gradually removing the obstacles which uphold intelligence to interfere with our supplying the place of those obstacles with others of a social nature which will accomplish all that the natural obstacles have done and in a better manner.

It is only in social affairs that the theory prevails that men should do nothing, that they should leave everything just as they happen to find it, and not try by the use of intelligence to improve on what has been given them by nature. We do not leave swamps undrained because water naturally stays there, nor do we suffer mad dogs to run loose because hydrophobia is the result of natural causes; neither should we fold our hands and allow a decline of intelligence because the course of natural events tends that way.

Considered by itself, it is not a cause for regret that the labor of the present is easier than that of the past, that machines do not need the skill of former times to tend them, and that production on a large scale is more mechanical and requires the use of much less intelligence. Nor is it a necessary misfortune that food is cheap and plenty, and that but little clothing is needed in warm countries. It is only when an easy mode of getting a living allows men to be careless and indolent, and permits the continuance of low social classes not otherwise possible, that these things, really beneficial under other conditions, become a curse.

The causes which assist the survival of the ignorant

K 19

arise from an exchange of services by which laborers do less than they would have to do if they lived in an isolated state,* while a few capitalists not only take care of themselves but also supply deficiencies of the laborers.

Capital, intelligence, skill, and manual labor are required to overcome the obstacles which are placed by nature between us and the things we desire. If every man were isolated, or so situated that he had in all respects to do his part towards surmounting these hinderances to the gratification of our desires, none could survive but those who had all the requisites for mastering the difficulties of nature.

In a new society, so long as every one is compelled from the necessities of the case to devote his whole energies to the care of himself and family, none can survive but those who have the requisite qualities. As soon as some persons have a surplus this can be and always is used to allow the introduction of social classes who are more or less deficient in the needed

---

* The term "isolated state" in this and following passages is not used in an absolute but in a relative sense, to denote that form of civilized society in which, owing to a lack of any extended division of labor and to the consequent imperfect development of exchange, each individual man must be able to produce, either alone or in connection with his immediate family, nearly all the different kinds of material commodities which he wishes to enjoy.

qualities, and who must rely upon others better equipped than themselves for mastering those difficulties which are insurmountable to the ignorant when by themselves. A few persons of skill and surplus capital form a combination with those who have only manual labor to offer in exchange for what they desire, and this combination is able to undersell competitors who combine their own skill and capital with their own labor. When this happens the accumulation of capital lowers the rate of interest to a minimum, and the rapid increase of population, which is always an accompaniment of ignorance, causes low wages.

If any society wishes to continue in a progressive state, the success of the combination just mentioned must be prevented by such social restrictions as will allow none to compete in the combinations of labor and capital except those who have the qualities that would enable them to survive in an isolated state, where they would of necessity depend entirely upon their own exertions. As intelligence, skill, and capital are necessary to overcome the difficulties placed about us by nature, the possession of these indispensable conditions to success should be required of all persons desiring employment, or enough more than the average of one of the conditions should be demanded to make up for deficiencies in regard to other conditions. If a person does not possess capital, more than ordinary intelligence and skill should be required of him; and if he does not possess them, he should be excluded from all places where he would through his deficiencies injure those who have prepared themselves in a proper manner to overcome the natural obstacles which interfere with our accomplishing what we desire. It is the want of such social restrictions that allows the gradual lowering of the rate of wages which accompanies the progress of civilization. In each new generation the relative number of those who possess the qualifications necessary to survive in an isolated state is reduced, and the average amount of the deficiencies of the laboring classes below the original standard is greatly increased. Every obstacle which, once surmounted, is forever set aside, every improvement which simplifies or lessens manual labor, every change in production from a smaller to a larger scale of operations, and every introduction of machinery which displaces skilled labor, increases the amount of the deficiencies which the laboring classes may possess without their being thereby overcome in the struggle for subsistence that the survival of the ignorant brings upon society.

There is but one way in which the gradual decline of wages can be prevented. In those occupations where the combinations of cheap labor and low interest are likely to succeed there should be required of all laborers seeking employment such tests of intelligence and skill as will exclude all classes below the average standard placed by nature for those who labor in an isolated condition and must possess in themselves all the requisites to success. If in a factory machinery is introduced by which a lower class of labor can be employed than formerly, society instead of allowing such persons to displace their betters should require that all subsequent laborers should have the same amount of intelligence and skill as was necessary in the case of those previously employed.

Ignorance and poverty will prevail among the laboring classes so long as no sufficient incentive is given these classes to increase their intelligence. If in a given factory the proportion of the unskilled labor to the skilled is ten to one, as is usually the case, ten of every eleven laborers can have no hope of promotion. Any amount of skill which they may possess will have no economic value to them, and as they have no inducement to become skilful they will remain in ignorance and poverty. Suppose now that from social restrictions none but skilled labor could be employed in the factory. In this case wages of skilled labor would have to be paid to all, and the ten unskilled men would now have a motive that would be sufficient to cause them to increase their skill and general intelligence up to the social standard. There are probably not five per cent. of the laboring population of any civilized country who would not willingly spend many years in preparing for their trade if thereby their future wages would be doubled. As it now is, if one parent keeps his children out of school he gains their wages, which another parent who sends his children to school loses. When these children, having become men, come into competition with one another the ignorant are at no disadvantage, since no test of intelligence is required.

The only advantage of the intelligent is that one in ten can obtain some recompense for the expense of his education by obtaining a position requiring skill and intelligence, and so long as this state of affairs continues there can be but one result,—nearly nine-tenths of the population will belong to the lowest classes of society, and will be a hinderance to all social progress.

Both a high rate of interest and high wages are necessary to preserve a high standard of life, and any plan of social improvement which would secure a high rate of wages by lowering interest is defective. A reduction of the rate of interest can only be accomplished by such a diminution of the inducement to save as will cause all capital to be concentrated in the hands of a few persons. A class of laborers who do not save for themselves will always be so deficient in intelligence as to lack those qualities necessary to maintain high wages, and they will necessarily sink to as low a social level as the surrounding natural conditions will allow. What is needed is that every one be required to do all his part, and that each one should obtain the whole reward which nature gives for labor and abstinence. So long as interest is low, and cheap labor is allowed to compete with skilled labor, the benefit of low interest does not come to the laborers, nor that of cheap labor to the capitalists, but the loss of both classes goes to the landlords, who reap all the benefits of low interest and cheap labor, no one receiving the whole of that reward which nature offers to those who save and labor. If intelligent laborers, who would save, had only to compete with the ignorant, who would not, the former could win in the contest everywhere; it is only when the latter are reinforced by low interest that they obtain the victory.

If this be true, then the endeavors of the state and the desires of the people to produce a low rate of interest are not favorable to the growth of capital and the prosperity of the country. The policy of the state should be rather to check the growth of that class of capital which is only loaned on safe investments, and encourage those classes of laborers who are willing to save if sufficient inducement is offered.

The state has ample power to do this, and that, too, without increasing the province of government by modifying the laws relating to property and the enforcement of contracts. All the powers of the government are now exerted to the uttermost to make all kinds of property safe investment and to enforce all kinds of contracts, on the grounds that these laws are necessary to encourage the growth of capital and lower the rate of interest. Of the kinds of capital which these laws encourage, most progressive nations have as much already as can find investment, and much more of this kind of capital could be had if employment for it could be found. For these reasons many of the present rigid laws for the enforcement of contracts could be modified and yet not reduce the amount of capital below what is needed.

For property there are two kinds of security, the one insuring to each producer the fruits of the industry obtained by his own exertions, and preventing other persons from appropriating these remunerations for labor without the owner's approval; the other security insures to the owner the return of property which with his consent has passed into the hands of others. These two propositions, that property should be protected and that contracts should be enforced, rest on very different grounds. The state cannot at the same time fully protect property and enforce all contracts. It is the purpose of most contracts to lower the rate of interest by giving the creditor better security, and where the rate of interest is low the increase of rent takes from every one a large part of that reward to which those who both labor and save have a just claim.

The need of protection of property is evident, and of it the government cannot furnish too great an amount; but the interests of the public suffer when the enforcement of contracts is not limited to those cases where it is plain the public is benefited. So long, for instance, as A tills a field himself the produce is his, and the laws should protect him in its possession. When, however, A yields possession of the land to B, on an agreement that B shall give him a share of the produce of his labor on the land, there are many reasons why the public welfare demands the enforcement of the contract. When B agrees to pay A a fixed sum for the use of the land, and if the produce is not sufficient to pay this rent A may take B's cattle, horses, or other capital, the reasons for the enforcement of this contract become less evident; but still less evident are these reasons when B agrees that A may take his future earnings to make up for a deficiency in the produce of the land. The enforcement of contracts has often been carried much further than in the above cases: creditors could put the debtors in jail, or sell them and their families as slaves, and sometimes the Shylock could demand even his pound of flesh.

Certainly all these means of enforcing contracts are

P

not now necessary, and an examination of the present laws for the protection of contracts will reveal many points where a modification would on economic grounds be desirable. At present the payment of all debts is enforced by law, and no difference is made whether the debtor is a laborer, a clerk, a farmer, or a merchant. Many classes never ought to be allowed to run into debt, and the best way to prevent it is not to allow certain debts to be enforced in the courts. It would be far better for the laborers to pay cash for what they purchase, instead of buying on credit and paying greatly increased prices at a later period. When this practice is once begun, they are in the power of the storekeepers if the state allows such contracts to be enforced. The garnishment of wages should not be allowed, even if the laborers really wished for it, and still less grounds are there for its enforcement when all the better classes of laborers oppose it. If the payment of such debts as are ordinarily secured by the garnishment of wages could not be enforced, only those laborers who had character and a sense of honor could obtain credit, and they would be just the ones who would not abuse the privilege. Besides, this would encourage the growth of societies among the laborers to assist and aid one another, and such societies could do more than the law can to aid sick and unfortunate workmen, and without the necessary misery which accompanies the enforced payment of debts by law.

The same course of reasoning shows that those who are not laborers in the narrow sense, such as clerks, salesmen, and professional men, would be better off if the right to enforce contracts against their salaries were taken away. They have no need of capital, and if they have not honor enough to pay their debts willingly, it is much better that they be deprived of the power to obtain the means of living extravagantly. It is easy to decide whether a man is engaged in some business requiring capital, and only those who need it for their business should the state encourage to obtain capital by means of a contract which the state agrees to enforce, and even in these cases the use of governmental power to enforce contracts should be confined to the narrowest limits.

It is only when both parties to the contract are engaged in some commercial enterprise where buying and selling form a legitimate part of their business that contracts should be strictly enforced by law. To such contracts there can be no objection on the ground that they favor cheap labor, and from them there is much advantage to be derived. Without a class of distributors whose contracts are enforced by law the advantages obtained from localizing industries in particular places, and the differences of soil and climate, cannot be utilized. The benefit derived from the enforcement of these contracts, however, does not prove that the state should allow its legal machinery to be used to oppress the industrial classes, who never ought to have had capital loaned them. The exchange of commodities between distant places adds largely to the efficiency of labor, but to no greater extent than does the act of producing before consuming on the part of all engaged in any industry. It is not expedient to trample down one harvest to reap another when a more discriminating method of procedure will enable both of them to be secured.

Whenever the enforcement of contracts enabling men to consume before they produce is lessened, the rate of interest rises, because more vigilance is required of creditors and less security given to them. This effect is much more than compensated for by the breaking up of the combination of cheap labor and low interest, by which the honorable and intelligent are driven entirely out of many departments, and much reduced in numbers in all others. The higher rate of interest induces all the people to save for themselves instead of borrowing, and capitalists as a class will vanish along with the low class of laborers by which they are sustained. A fall of the rate of interest is a sign that capital is not fulfilling its proper economic function of extending production, and that the nation can get its supply of capital without submitting to as hard terms as formerly, and better terms should be preferred to a low rate of interest and the disastrous consequences in which it is sure to involve the whole nation.

In all productive enterprises there is considerable risk. Some years the crops are better than others, railroads and ships do not always have the same amount of goods to transport, and the producers of manufactured commodities do not find as ready sales for their products at one time as at another. Although these risks are very much greater in one occupation than in others, yet there is always some risk in every productive undertaking, and the question necessarily arises, Who shall bear the risk? According to the method of division of profits usually pursued in factories and other corporations, a certain rate of interest is given for as much capital as can be securely invested, and the rest of the capital is held by the stockholders or partners, who assume all risks. In this way the losses are borne and the extra gains are secured by a very few persons, and from such an arrangement there can be but one result. The laborers and the mass of the capitalists who seek safe investments will have much less intelligence, and thus interest and wages will sink to a lower point than would be the case were all the interested parties compelled to assume their share of the risk.

20

The division of capital into two classes—safe and unsafe investments, or bonds and stocks, as they are commonly called—causes the cautious classes of capitalists to prefer bonds, while the sanguine and adventurous persons take the stocks and have the entire control of industry. Such men, naturally bold and reckless, tend strongly to speculation rather than to legitimate enterprise, since greater immediate profit is often obtained by the former than by the latter means. In any nation where the more daring portion of the capitalists are allowed to assume all the risk of every enterprise there will be sure to grow up a class loving such risks, and the business of the country will be turned from the most substantial investments for capital to those most hazardous, yet offering a chance for a few to make a great gain. Daring capitalists may prefer a small gross profit in a hazardous enterprise, most of which will be obtained by the few who are successful, to a safe investment offering a much greater gross return ; but surely this speculative spirit is not what the public welfare demands. Most of the industries of a country will always be in dangerous hands so long as two-thirds of the capital engaged in them is in bonds or notes and the stock is again given as security for the greater part of its value. The prosperity of the people demands that all capitalists, and even laborers, should bear their share of the risks in-

cident to all productive enterprises, and receive a part
of the extra gains. If all of the capital of any cor-
poration were in stock, and this stock could not be
given as security on which to borrow more money,
much the greater part of speculation would be done
away with. The more conservative capitalist now
holding bonds would then have a voice in the manage-
ment of the affairs of the company, while the more
daring persons, now inclined to take risks, would be
limited to their own capital, and thus could speculate
much less than at present, when by giving their stock
as security they can often obtain an amount of stock
five or six times that of their capital. Speculation
can only be limited by greatly increasing the proportion of stocks to the safe investments, such as bonds
and notes, and by limiting the amount for which stock
or other property can be given as security to a very low
per cent. of its value.

The extent of the injury which a strict enforcement
of contracts brings to a nation is largely determined
by the stability of the value of commodities. Where
the fluctuations of values are small and infrequent,
the injury is much less than when large and frequent
changes in values cause the return for labor to be so
uncertain that all industry becomes largely a matter
of speculation. The more extended use of land having
great obstructions to its cultivation, production on a

large scale, and the many evils arising from the use of cheap labor and low interest, all tend to increase the fluctuations of values, and to destroy the stability of the value of the precious metals used as money by the whole world. From these causes the risks of all productive enterprises have in the past gradually increased, and they will soon be so great that a small indebtedness may ruin the most cautious producer if the enforcement of contracts is not limited, and every one engaged in production compelled to assume his proper share of the risk.

The reason usually assigned for not limiting the power of contracting debts is, that by this means the capital of a country gets into the most efficient hands. Certainly it is often true that the efficiency of capital is thus increased, but surely capital is not best utilized when nine-tenths of it is out of the control of those by whom it has been saved.

In former times, when the tendency to save was weak and the disinclination to lend capital was strong, the enforcement of contracts did add much to the efficiency of the small amount of capital which the nation possessed. At the present time, however, there is no lack of capital for those industries where the scale of production is large enough to offer security to those seeking safe investments. If further progress is made, it must be accomplished by favoring those who, saving for themselves, will utilize the many opportunities to labor which production on a large scale has not developed. The enforcement of contracts adds to the efficiency of the surplus capital which cannot be employed in the possessor's own business, but it reduces the return on the capital which the owner uses himself. Safe investments, therefore, should be encouraged when but few are willing to save. The extra security, however, should be gradually withdrawn as the rate of interest falls, so that a greater number of persons will have sufficient inducement to save and become skilled. By this method alone can all those opportunities to labor be utilized which require for their development a skilled workman who saves for himself. The state should not prevent all safe investments, but it should limit them, so as to cause all necessary risks to be borne by as large a part of the producers as possible.

Whenever the government enforces all contracts the creditors rely too much on the power of the state, and do not use that vigilance that would otherwise be necessary. The capitalists becoming less intelligent when thus patronized by the state, seek only safe investments, such as bonds and mortgages, while the same influences lower the moral standard of the debtors, since capitalists would as soon lend to dishonorable as to honorable men if there is a chance to protect their interests by legal means. That society could exist and prosper without contracts being enforced by the government to any extent is well illustrated in the United States, where, on account of the expense, delay, and uncertainty of justice, many classes of capitalists are forced to be careful that none of their money gets into dishonest hands and use that vigilance which would be necessary if no enforced debts were allowed by law.

Wherever capitalists must rely more on themselves than on the laws, commerce and trade are in a better condition and the rate of profit better than in those industries where the laws can be fully enforced. Agriculture forms the best example for showing the evil results of capitalists relying on the law. The crops of the farmer mature only at certain seasons of 'the year, and whatever he has is in plain sight and cannot be removed. For these reasons a dishonest man can be placed on a farm, and easily watched and prevented from escaping without the payment of rent or interest. Whenever the honest and intelligent farmer must compete with the low and ignorant of his class, aided by an absentee capitalist, the combination of ignorance and capital held together by the force of the law always in the end succeeds. Those having a low rate of interest and cheap labor can pay a higher price for land than the intelligent, upright farmer, who needs high wages and interest in order to have sufficient inducement to live and bring up a family who are not a dishonor to the nation. If the agricultural classes are ever made to prosper, it can only be done by such limitations of the power to enforce contracts and the rights of property in land as will make it unprofitable to let any but the strictly honest and intelligent occupy farms. Then there will be a higher rate of profit and a great increase of produce and a general improvement of the agricultural classes.

In many States of the Union important steps have been taken in the right direction by enacting exemption laws and giving homestead rights to the occupant. These laws will be of little importance, however, so long as the parties interested are allowed to sign away their rights, since the very classes which should be prevented from obtaining possession of the land are always willing to sign away all rights and thus defeat the purpose of the act.

The principle which should be recognized in laws protecting the agricultural as well as all other classes of producers is, that no one should have a legal right to pledge the produce of his own labor before he has produced it. The share of annual produce of the country due to the laborers should be reserved for them, and the law should not take any one's share from his possession on account of any contract made before the work is performed, nor should the law enforce any lien on the annual produce of industry that will reduce the share that should go to the laborers. The right to mortgage or rent land should be so limited that there will be enough produce remaining to give those who labor on the land their part of the annual produce, and no agreement which allows rent or interest to absorb the laborer's share should be enforced. Natural causes will not allow any class to survive who consume before they produce, and all laws which allow this to be done are detrimental to public welfare. Instead of consuming months before they produce, the laborers should produce months before they consume. It is a law of nature that labor performed before the commodity is needed will greatly increase the produce, and no social regulation should allow those who consume before they produce to displace those who conform to what nature demands. The laws which aid those who consume before they produce are said to aid poor men, but if properly examined it will be seen that such laws do not aid poor men, they make poor men. The correct method of aiding the poor and unfortunate is in the formation of societies among the laborers for that purpose, and in this way those who deserve aid can get it. To allow laws favoring ignorant and improvident men to be enforced, causes the displacement of both the honest laborer and those poor men who really deserve aid, by a lower class of laborers not willing to conform to natural laws. Any one who consumes before he produces is a slave of some one else, and no free man should be compelled to compete with slave labor. The poor and the rich are always found in combination, and when no legal obstacles are placed in the way of the success of this combination, they will force the price of labor so low and that of food so high as to drive out the independent and intelligent laborers who would furnish their own capital and thus make co-operation a success. It is only where tests of intelligence prevent the employment of cheap labor, and where limitations to the enforcement of contracts and the right of inheritance prevent the fall of interest, that this combination can be displaced by men who conform to nature enough to be really free ; and no one is really free but he who possesses such qualifications as would enable him to survive if he were placed in an isolated state where he would be compelled to supply all his wants. When this is done poverty and ignorance will no longer increase as civilization progresses, and each man will obtain all the reward which nature gives in return for intelligence, labor, and abstinence.

For the preservation of a high standard of life more than a high rate of interest and wages is necessary. Mankind has a tendency to increase, and this increase must be provided for by an extension of cultivation. Although the tendency to increase is reduced as man conforms more and more to the demands of nature and thus acquires increased means of enjoyment, yet the enlarged population must be provided for, or society will sink to a lower social state, where the higher rate of increase will be required to replace the greater losses through premature deaths, due to the less favorable surroundings. The growth of population compels mankind either to progress or retrograde; there is no available middle course; either through an extension of the field of·employment the wants of all men must be provided for, or the evils of an unequal distribution of wealth will reduce the efficiency of labor and cause man to fall back to a prior social state. An extension of production, however, would of itself be desirable even if there were no necessity forcing man in this direction. The obstacles to cultivation when once surmounted do not cause additional proportional labor to be used in tilling the new land, while the more varied consumption and the enlarged capacities of enjoyment, which always accompany a greater conformity to nature, increase the pleasures of life without adding to its burdens.

The means which thus far have been used to procure an extension of the field of employment are costly and wasteful in their operation, and by causing an unequal distribution of wealth usually prevent the very result they are supposed to accomplish. When the state makes no provision for the extension of cultivation, it must be brought about by a diminution of the return for labor and capital in the field of employment already occupied below the immediate return on the new land. In this manner labor and capital are induced to leave their old industries and displace the obstacles which prevent the use of new land. Suppose that of every twenty acres ten are already in use, the price of the produce being fifty cents per bushel, and that fifty-five cents a bushel are required to bring the eleventh acre into cultivation, sixty cents for the twelfth acre, and a like increase of price for the others. With free competition the price of produce must rise to fifty-five cents a bushel before the eleventh acre will be tilled. On ten of the eleven acres now used the cost of production has not risen, and the additional five cents a bushel on all their produce goes to the owners as rent. The people pay eleven times as much for the additional produce as they would have paid if they had anticipated the increase in price of produce and prevented it by bringing the new land into cultivation at public expense. When the twelfth acre is brought into use the public pay twelve times what is necessary for this purpose, and a proportionally greater amount for the other acres. They also pay permanently for what requires but a temporary outlay, since the extra cost is only necessary while the land is being prepared for tillage, yet under free competition the price must continue to rise, so that produce may be obtained from other lands having a greater cost of preparation.

The only economic method for any society to pursue is to anticipate the rise of rent and use the public revenue to overcome the obstacles to the extension of the field of employment. Even if taxation reduced the earnings of labor, it would be better to have a small reduction in this way than the much larger reduction of wages which the rise of rent would otherwise occasion. There is, however, no reason to believe that an increase of taxation would be a burden upon the laborers, since it would reduce rent, if there is no land at the margin of cultivation.

The advocates of the nationalization of land, who demand that all taxes be placed on rent, base their doctrine on the truth of the Ricardian theory of rent, which asserts that there is always some land at the margin of cultivation which pays no rent, and will be thrown out of cultivation if the price of agricultural produce is lowered. When all land pays rent, any permanent tax will reduce rent, since it will change the ratio at which food exchanges for other commodities. If ten yards of cloth exchange for a bushel of wheat, and a tax equal to the value of one yard is laid, either on cloth or food, it will be paid from rent so long as the exchange of nine yards of cloth for a bushel of wheat does not reduce the quantity of wheat produced. Rent should be anticipated and prevented, but not confiscated. There never has been guaranteed any permanent ratio of exchange between agricultural produce and other commodities, and if the people use legitimate means to bring about a ratio of exchange more favorable to themselves, the landlords have no right to complain. The obstacles to the extension of production, whether in men or land, must be removed even if at public expense, or the people can enjoy but few pleasures, while land and intelligence will be monopolies, and absorb the larger share of the produce of industry.

The removal of the obstacles in land is greatly surpassed in importance by the public utility of a correct system of education displacing the obstacles to the increase of intelligence. Even the obstacles to cultivating land arise mainly from ignorance and prejudice, and are removed by the broader view of life which education brings to its possessors. It is upon education alone that we can rely for increasing the efficiency of labor, and bringing out all the qualities in land and man which are necessary to adjust man to the conditions of nature, and open up to him all the means of enjoyment which nature offers to those who conform to all her demands.

In the original man only his passions and appetites

L   q   21

are active, while all the other sources of pleasure are unavailable, since their appreciation depends upon qualities not as yet called into exercise. Each different occupation develops some quality which adds to its possessor's sources of pleasure. The nations which follow the chase as a means of support derive their pleasures from this source; nomadic tribes delight in horsemanship and other similar sports; warlike nations enjoy archery, hunting, and fencing; the agricultural classes have resources of happiness closely connected with their surroundings, and the individuals of each class in every other occupation take their pleasures from sources which their active qualities allow them to enjoy.

The man whose vocation calls into activity but one quality has but few sources of pleasure, and in him the tendency to overpopulate, to eat, and to drink is so strong as to injure himself and society. It is to such men, and not to those with fully-developed faculties, that Malthus refers to prove the universality of his law, and there is a seeming justification for this position when we see how universally the combinations of weak men, with but one active quality, displace the strong men, who have developed all the qualities given them by nature. Wherever an extended division of labor is carried through there is a combination of men, each having only one quality developed, and relying on those having some other active quality to make up his deficiencies. They all desire only physical pleasures, and the field of employment is limited by the unequal distribution of wealth which they are sure to bring upon themselves. The greater the number of qualities which are developed in any man the more sources of pleasure will he have, and the greater will be the inducement to labor and to control his physical pleasures, so that he may have the means of enjoying all that his developed faculties allow him to appreciate.

Man's power to enjoy is commensurate with his power to produce, and there are no means of enlarging our sources of pleasure but by increasing our industrial efficiency. It is not the man who can do one thing well, but he who is efficient in many directions, that has the most resources for obtaining happiness. The injuries accompanying the division of labor arise from each man's devoting himself so exclusively to one occupation that he loses both the power to make and to enjoy what others produce. When each person can perform all the acts necessary in an isolated state, it increases the efficiency of all if one becomes a tailor, the second a spinner, the third a shoemaker, and so on, the others taking those vocations in which they are most efficient. Each one, however, following his trade exclusively, loses his power to make anything else, and also his ability to enjoy what he formerly produced, and thus the whole society sinks to a lower social state, where physical pleasures are the sole means of enjoyment. The increase of drunkenness and other physical vices which have accompanied modern progress are the result of the extended division of labor, which destroys the ability both to produce and to enjoy most of those things that are sources of pleasure to man in an isolated state. We can obtain the advantage derived from the division of labor without losing the ability to enjoy all kinds of produce only by so educating all the faculties of man that he will have that independence and all those sources of pleasure which isolated men enjoy. Moreover, those qualities which increase the sources of pleasure are the very ones by which the field of employment is enlarged and the tendency to overpopulate is reduced, and only when education has developed all the qualities in every man can we expect this tendency to become so harmless that all men can enjoy the pleasures of an isolated state along with the efficiency of modern civilization.

THE END.

www.ingramcontent.com/pod-product-compliance
Lightning Source LLC
Chambersburg PA
CBHW020856270326
41928CB00006B/724